BIG BOOK OF
INTARSIA
WOODWORKING

The Best of **SCROLLSAW**
Woodworking & Crafts Magazine

BIG BOOK OF
INTARSIA
WOODWORKING

**37 Projects and Expert Techniques
for Segmentation and Intarsia**

From the Editors of *Scroll Saw*
Woodworking & Crafts

FOX CHAPEL
PUBLISHING

Cover art: *Lighthouse Scene* by Janette Square, page 64.
Page 2 art: *Raccoon* by Judy Gale Roberts and Jerry Booher, page 140.

© 2011 by Fox Chapel Publishing Company, Inc., East Petersburg, PA.

Patterns on pages 29, 30, 62, 63, 72, 73, 78, 79, 85, 86, 87, 97, 98, 103, 104, 105, 131, 136, 137, 156, 157, 164, and 165 © 2011 by Kathy Wise Designs Inc.

ISBN 978-1-56523-550-2

Library of Congress Cataloging-in-Publication Data

BIG BOOK OF INTARSIA WOODWORKING / From the editors of Scroll Saw Woodworking & Crafts.

    pages cm. -- (The Best of Scroll Saw Woodworking & Crafts Magazine)

Includes index.

ISBN 978-1-56523-550-2

1. Marquetry. 2. Woodwork--Patterns. I. Scroll saw woodworking & crafts.

TT192.B54 2011

745.51'2--dc22

      2010047877

To learn more about the other great books from Fox Chapel Publishing, or to find a retailer near you, call toll-free 800-457-9112 or visit us at *www.FoxChapelPublishing.com*.

Note to Authors: We are always looking for talented authors to write new books in our area of woodworking, design, and related crafts. Please send a brief letter describing your idea to Acquisition Editor, 1970 Broad Street, East Petersburg, PA 17520.

Printed in China
First printing: May 2011

Table of Contents

What You Can Make

Flowers and Scenes

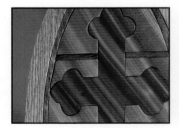
Stained glass, page 12

Calla lillies, page 22

Blossoms, page 38

Rose, page 39

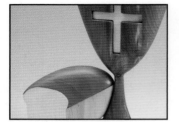
Cup and loaf, page 40

Magnolia door topper,
page 44

Seaside scene, page 51

Sunflower wreath, page 58

Lighthouse, page 64

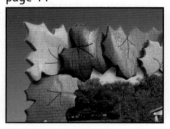
Leaf frame page 69

Rose frame, page 74

Scarecrow, page 88

Birds

Macaw, page 16

Duck, page 25

Turkey, page 80

Cardinal frame, page 96

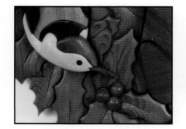
Birds and berries wreath,
page 99

Toucan, page 118

Chickadee, page 122

Toucan, page 124

Birds *(continued)*

Woodpecker, page 138

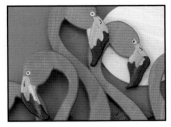
Flamingos, page 145

Pelican, page 166

Songbirds, page 184

Animals

Bunnies, page 36

Puppy, page 108

Cat magnets, page 115

Squirrel, page 130

Arabian horse, page 132

Raccoon, page 140

Fox, page 150

Colt, page 152

Raccoon, page 158

Cat, page 160

Bobcat, page 169

Pony, page 175

Elephant, page 180

Techniques

Whether you're a beginner or veteran in the world of intarsia, there's no better way to learn than from someone else's experience.

In this chapter, you will find step-by-step instructions from a 17-year-old who creates his own designs and from a professional who enhances her artwork with acrylic paint and food coloring. There's more from a couple who have discovered how much careful grain placement can improve a project and another professional who crafts inlaid frames to display his masterpieces.

You will finish these lessons with more to be proud of than just new skills—your very own works of art!

Finally, if you just need some expert advice, there's a handy chart to help you select the best wood for your needs and a question-and-answer session with an acknowledged master of the craft, Judy Gale Roberts, who addresses issues from which tools to use to how to handle mistakes.

Original design by Nick Berchtold, page 23.

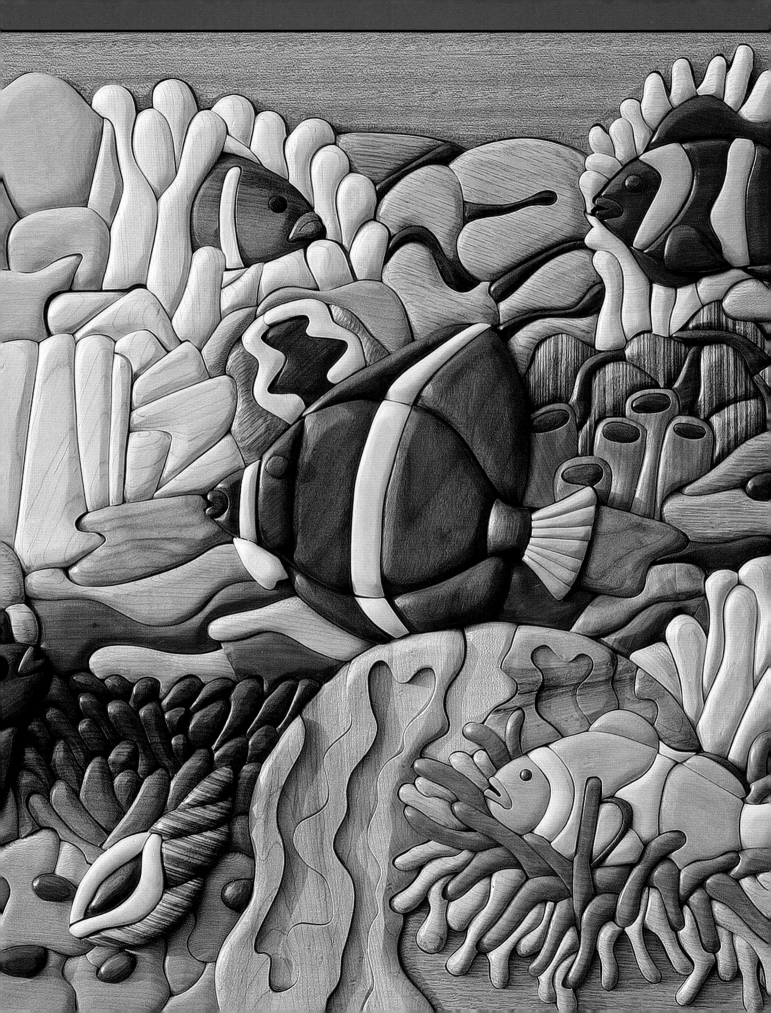

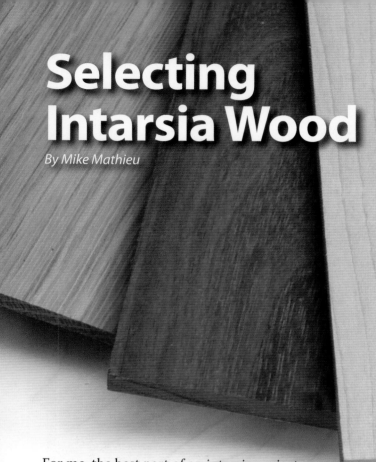

Selecting Intarsia Wood

By Mike Mathieu

For me, the best part of an intarsia project is picking out the wood to use. I spend hours matching up different colors and figures of wood. Often, woodworkers don't realize the vibrant wood they use in their project will change over time. Careful wood selection and a knowledge of how aging affects the color of specific woods will help your intarsia project stand the test of time.

I have been very fortunate to be able to use many different types of woods in my intarsia. I have learned a lot about the color changes wood goes through as it ages. When I created my first rose box, I used pink ivory for the rose. It was the most beautiful wood I had ever seen, and it made the perfect rose. Unfortunately, pink ivory turns brown. I did some research and found bloodwood. As the name implies, the wood is red, and best of all, it stays red.

To save you the expense of choosing wood through trial and error, I'm sharing what I have learned from experience. Please note this is not a complete list, but it does provide a range of colors to help you make the most of your intarsia projects.

A printable chart is available here:
www.scrollsawer.com/techniques/selecting-intarsia-wood.html

Species	Color and figure	Intarsia uses	Effects of time
African padauk	reddish orange	orange background wood	darkens with age
American walnut	nice brown color	good general dark wood	no change
Apple	tan	flesh tone	darkens with age
Ash	wide open grain, light with tan stripes	landscape	no change
Bird's-eye maple	light tan	great accent wood	slight darkening with age
Bloodwood	red	anything red	no change
Bubinga	brick red with wild grain	good general wood	no change

Species	Color and figure	Intarsia uses	Effects of time
Canarywood	yellow with orange streaks	great accent wood	darkens with age
Cherry	reddish tan	frames and boxes	darkens with age
Cocobolo	wild grain, variety of color and shades	good background wood	darkens with age
Ebony	black	anything black	no change
Fishtail oak	reddish brown, unique grain	tree trunks, bird feathers	no change
Holly	almost pure white, tight grain	anything white	no change
Honduran mahogany	nice grain, reddish brown	frames, boxes	darkens with age
Ipe	greenish brown	background	darkens with age
Jatoba	nice grain, reddish brown	background	darkens with age
Kingwood	purple with black stripes, wild grain	background	darkens with age
Lacewood	light brown to silver, unique grain	water, bird feathers	no change
Hard maple	light tan	good general wood	darkens slightly

Species	Color and figure	Intarsia uses	Effects of time
Osage-orange	bright yellow	not recommended due to change	turns dark brown
Pau amarillo	yellow	fall leaves, anything yellow	no change
Pear	peach color	flesh tone	darkens with age
Pernambuco	bright orange with black stripes, rare	anything orange, fall leaves	no change
Persimmon	light tan with tight grain	cloudy skies	no change
Peruvian walnut	uniform chocolate color, nice grain	anything brown	no change
Poplar (green)	variety of shades available	anything green, trees	may darken to brown with age
Purpleheart	purple	mountain tops, anything purple	darkens with age
Sycamore	tan, light unique grain	feathers on birds	holds color well
Tulipwood	red on creamy background, beautiful grain	sunset, sunrise, flower petals	no change
Wenge	black with brown stripes, coarse	good dark wood	no change
Zebrawood	black lines against tan background	good background wood	darkens slightly

Create Stunning Effects with Wood Grain

By Carol and Homer Bishop

Intarsia projects rely on different woods to produce the desired effect. The same pattern can result in two different projects depending on the wood selection. While the color of each section is important, the figure or pattern created by the wood grain is a critical aspect that is often overlooked.

This design relies heavily on the pattern of the grain to simulate sunlight streaming through the window. While the design itself is fairly simple, the end result will be lackluster without careful attention to the direction of the grain in the wood you select.

1 **Cut the frame and leading.**
Attach copies of the pattern to the frame stock and the leading stock with spray adhesive. We cut the frame from oak. Leading is the metal used to connect the panes in a stained glass window. We chose blue pine for the leading. Position the cut pieces on a copy of the pattern.

2 **Cut the cross window panel.**
Orient the grain of the aromatic red cedar diagonally across the cross to create the effect of sunlight streaming in through the window. Attach the pattern to the cedar and cut the piece. This same angle must be maintained on all other glass pieces to create a realistic effect.

3 **Cut the lighter window panels.**
Lay the cut cross piece on top of the wood for the other panels. Match the stripes in the Western red cedar with the stripes in the aromatic cedar. Move the cross around looking for the best fit. Match each individual panel to the cross and transfer the pattern to the wood.

4 **Check the fit of the pieces.** Clamp the pieces together to ensure a good fit. If the grain patterns do not match up or there are gaps between cut pieces, cut a new piece. The overall appeal of the piece depends on the pattern of the grain lining up across all panels of the window.

5 **Finish the stained glass project.**
Sand and shape the pieces as desired. Glue and clamp the pieces together using wood glue. Allow the glue to dry and then apply varnish or your finish of choice. Add a hanger to the back and remember to sign your work.

Materials & Tools

Materials:
- ¾" x 3" x 13" oak or wood of choice (frame)
- ¾" x 8" x 8½" aromatic red cedar (cross panel)
- ¾" x 3" x 20" Western red cedar (light panels)
- ¾" x 2½" x 11¼" blue pine (window leading)
- Spray adhesive
- Wood glue
- Varnish or finish of choice
- Hanger

Tools:
- #4 skip-tooth blades
- Drum sander
- Flap sander

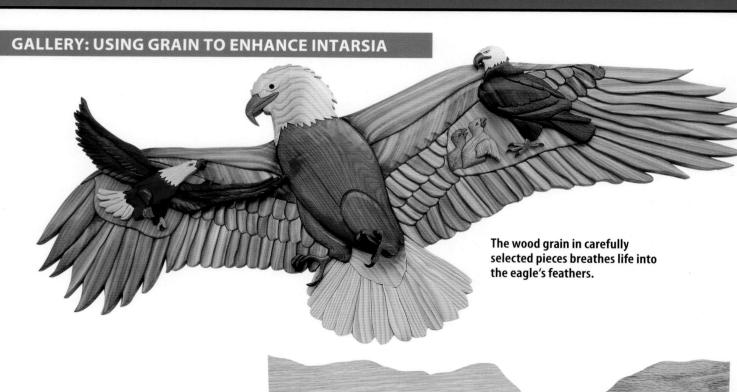

The wood grain in carefully selected pieces breathes life into the eagle's feathers.

Strategic pattern placement around a knot gives the illusion of flowing water and the fisherman's shadow.

The distinctive grain around Jesus' feet simulates ripples in the water.

Photocopy at 100%

Adding Color to Intarsia

By Kathy Wise

I prefer to use natural wood colors for my intarsia projects, but sometimes a piece requires an unavailable or impossible-to-find color. Because bright blue wood is not available, I use acrylic paint washes and food coloring to achieve the characteristic colors on this beautiful intarsia macaw.

I add the black markings to the face with a wood burner. Test the blue dye or acrylic paint washes on several types of wood to determine which look you prefer. Let the colored wood dry overnight and apply varnish or your top coat of choice to see exactly how the color will look. For an easier project, cut this pattern from one piece of wood and stain or dye all of the pieces.

Start by making six copies of the pattern. Keep a master copy for future use. Cut the pattern apart and separate the pieces into color groups. Tape contact paper flat on a board. Spray adhesive on the pattern pieces and position them on the shiny side of the contact paper. Cut the pieces adhered to the contact paper apart, peel the backing off the contact paper, and stick them on the wood. Follow the grain direction arrows.

TIP   MIXING COLORS

Test your paint or dye on several pieces of wood to determine which wood and concentration of paint or dye will look best. You want the wood figure to show through the color. I used sycamore for the blue parts of the macaw because it has a nice figure that shows through the paint wash.

To make a wash, add a small amount of water to ultramarine blue acrylic paint. Additional coats of the paint wash will intensify the color. Write down the ratio of paint to water for later reference.

Food coloring mixed with water is another option for adding color to your work. I used this method to intensify the bright gold of the macaw. You could also use green dye or paint to enhance the leaves.

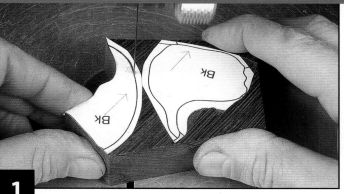

1 **Cut the main sections.** I use a #5 skip-tooth blade. Make sure your blade is square to the saw table by using a square to check a cut piece. Plane any wood that is not flat. Number the back of each cut piece with a pencil. Do not divide the individual pieces cut from the same color of wood.

2 **Cut the eyeball.** Drill a ⅛"-diameter hole for the pupil. Sand a small piece of ebony into a ⅛"-diameter dowel by holding it against the drum sander with pliers. Glue the dowel into the hole. Cut the dowel flush with the surface and then cut the white of the eye. Round the eyeball on the drum sander.

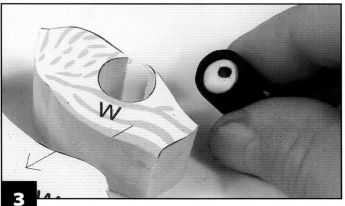

3 **Finish the eye.** Drill a blade-entry hole in the center of the black ring around the eye and cut the center hole. Then cut the perimeter and test the fit of the eyeball. Cut the adjoining face piece and test the fit of the black ring.

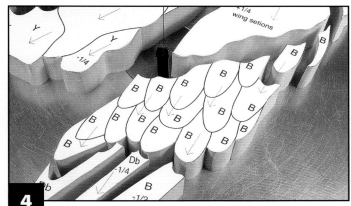

4 **Cut the feathers and individual pieces.** Use a #3 skip-tooth blade to cut the individual feathers. The smaller blade gives you a smaller kerf so the pieces will fit together better. Use the same blade to divide the yellow belly section.

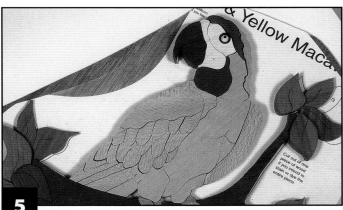

5 **Dry fit the pieces.** Position the cut pieces on a full-size pattern taped to a piece of plywood. Check the fit of the pieces and adjust as needed. If you do not like the wood color or grain of the pieces, change them now.

6 **Adjust the fit of the pieces.** Practice on scrap wood first. Hold two pieces together and recut along the line with a #3 blade. You may have to recut the line a few times, but each cut will draw the pieces closer together.

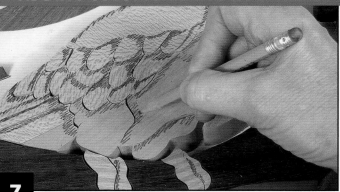

7 **Prepare to shape the pieces.** Shade the deepest areas using the shaping guide as a reference. I use an 8"-diameter drum equipped with 120-grit sandpaper for fast wood removal and a 2"-diameter drum equipped with 220-grit sandpaper for the final sanding. Work slowly and constantly replace your pieces next to adjoining pieces to check your progress.

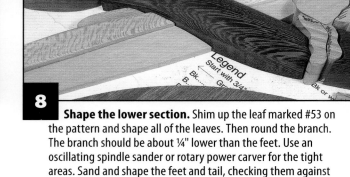

8 **Shape the lower section.** Shim up the leaf marked #53 on the pattern and shape all of the leaves. Then round the branch. The branch should be about ¼" lower than the feet. Use an oscillating spindle sander or rotary power carver for the tight areas. Sand and shape the feet and tail, checking them against the branch. The branch is below the feet, but above the tail.

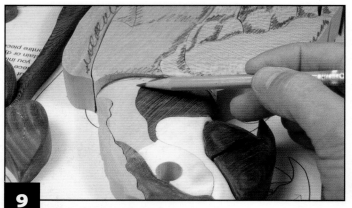

9 **Finish shaping the bird.** Use shaped pieces to mark the sanding depth on surrounding pieces. Remove a lot of wood between the upper and lower beak. Hold one or two feathers together and sand the top edge of the entire group of feathers. Put a sharp angle on each feather.

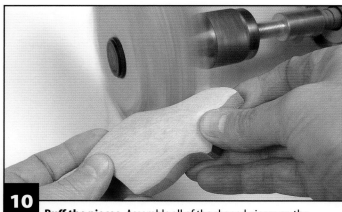

10 **Buff the pieces.** Assemble all of the shaped pieces on the full-size pattern and check for fit and flow. Make any necessary adjustments. Use a 220-grit sanding mop to buff each piece. The mop gives the pieces a nice sheen and makes it easier to apply a smooth coat of finish.

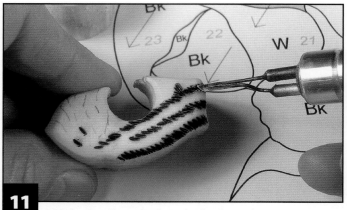

11 **Add the details to the face.** Apply white gel stain to the white areas of the face. Use a woodburner to add the black feathery lines around the eye using the gray lines on the pattern as a guide. Use a woodburner to add small texture lines to the feet and around the edges of the black eye ring.

12 **Add the color.** Use diluted yellow food coloring on the yellow pieces. Apply two coats of the blue paint wash to the light blue areas and three coats to the dark blue areas. Let the pieces dry overnight. If the grain raises, rub the pieces lightly with fine steel wool, sandpaper, or a paper bag.

13 **Cut the backing board.** Glue the macaw pieces into three sections using cyanoacrylate (CA) glue. Sand the bottom flat for a level gluing surface. Trace the outline of the macaw onto a piece of ¼"-thick plywood or hardboard for a backing board. Cut ¹⁄₁₆" inside the lines. Sand the edges of the backing board with the sanding mop and paint the edges and back black.

14 **Glue the project to the backing board.** Place the three sections in position on the backing board. Lift one section and add dots of wood glue to the backing board. Then add a few drops of CA glue between the wood glue. Replace the section of the macaw and press firmly until the CA glue sets up. Use the same process to glue down the two other sections.

15 **Finish the macaw.** Trim any overhanging backer board and touch up the paint on the edges. Apply several coats of spray varnish or your finish of choice to the intarsia. Allow the finish to dry overnight. Cover the macaw's eye with clear glossy finish for a lifelike shine. Attach a mirror-style hanger to the back.

Materials & Tools

Materials:
These are the woods I use; you can use your woods of choice.
- 1" x 8" x 17" dark wood such as wenge (branch and beak)
- 1" x 9" x 4" yellow wood such as yellowheart or satinwood (breast and tail)
- ½" x 5" x 5" gray wood such as blue pine (feet)
- ¼" x 2" x 2" black wood such as ebony (eye)
- 1" x 7" x 10" light wood such as sycamore (feathers, stained blue)
- 1" x 2½" x 2½" white wood such as poplar (face)
- 1" x 6" x 7" green wood such as lignum vitae (leaves)
- ½" x 12" x 4" light wood such as sycamore (feathers, stained blue)

- ¼" x 15" x 22" plywood or hardboard (backing board)
- Roll of clear contact paper
- Spray adhesive
- Wood glue
- Cyanoacrylate glue and accelerator
- Spray varnish
- Mirror-style hanger
- Blue & yellow paint or dye

Tools:
- #3 and #5 skip-tooth blades or blades of choice
- Drill press or drill with ¹¹⁄₆₄"-diameter drill bit
- Pneumatic-drum sander with 120- and 220-grit sanding drums
- 220-grit sanding mop

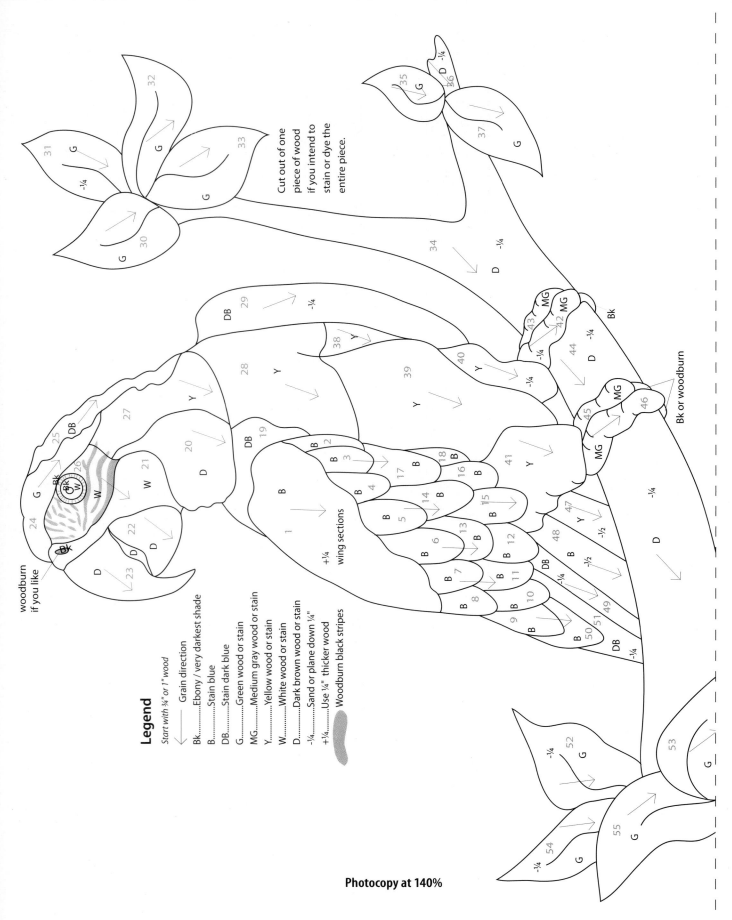

Cut out of one
piece of wood
if you intend to
stain or dye the
entire piece.

woodburn
if you like

Legend

Start with ¾" or 1" wood

→...........Grain direction

Bk...........Ebony / very darkest shade

B...........Stain blue

DB...........Stain dark blue

G...........Green wood or stain

MG...........Medium gray wood or stain

Y...........Yellow wood or stain

W...........White wood or stain

D...........Dark brown wood or stain

-¼...........Sand or plane down ¼"

+¼...........Use ¼" thicker wood

🬀...........Woodburn black stripes

Bk or woodburn

Photocopy at 140%

Shaping Guide

Photocopy at 140%

Designing Intarsia Patterns

By Nick Berchtold

I was 16 when I touched my first scroll saw—and I haven't been able to keep my hands off it since. My father set up his saw in 2004 and I started cutting fretwork patterns. To keep myself challenged, I started cutting larger projects and then moved on to intarsia—and those projects have progressively gotten bigger as well.

I started designing my own patterns because I always ended up changing commercial patterns anyway.

After a while, I just started sketching my own. I design custom pieces on commission, but in my free time, I design patterns for the sheer joy of it.

When designing patterns, I leave them very basic at first. I fill in the detail as I go along, so none of my pieces are ever the same. I find the cutting goes pretty quickly; most of my time is spent in the shaping.

Legend

A .... Aspen
B .... Padauk
C .... Cherry
M .... Maple
N .... Pine
P .... Poplar
W .... Walnut

Just 17 years old, Nick Berchtold both designed and created this calla lilly intarsia.

Step 1: Prepare your stock. Make a copy of the original pattern, so you have one to refer to. Attach the pattern pieces to your wood of choice.

Step 2: Cut out the pieces.

Step 3: Cut or sand the pieces to the desired depth. Once pieces are all cut out and fitted properly, I re-saw the pieces of the flowers and background to the desired depth with the band saw. It is possible to sand these pieces to the desired depth, but it takes longer.

Step 4: Rough sand the pieces. Sand them until they all flow together. Then sand the pieces with progressively finer grits of sandpaper.

Step 5: Glue the pieces together. Use your wood glue of choice.

Step 6: Prepare a frame. Make a frame with a routed-out back so you can glue a backer board in, or purchase a frame that is ⅛6" larger on all sides of the intarsia. Glue the backer board into the frame.

Step 7: Glue the intarsia to the backer board in the frame.

Step 8: Apply two to three coats of a clear finish to the project.

Several of Nick's original intarsia designs.

Materials & Tools

Materials:
- Double-sided tape or spray adhesive
- Clear finish of choice
- Wood glue

Woods:
- ½" poplar
- ¼" pine
- Following woods in ¾": maple, padauk, aspen, walnut, cherry

Tools:
- #9 skip-tooth blades or blades of choice
- Band saw (optional)
- Sander of choice (I use a pneumatic sanding drum, an oscillating spindle sander, and a mop sander)

Photocopy at 120%

Creating a Custom Inlay Frame

By Mike Mathieu

While some intarsia projects are designed to stand alone, I prefer to frame my rectangular pieces. The frame gives the intarsia a professional, finished look.

This custom frame incorporates a strip of walnut inlay to complement the intarsia. Overlaying intarsia elements on top of the frame adds depth and interest to the presentation.

1

Prepare the frame stock. Cut the frame stock to the final dimensions as you cut the 45° miters. The inside dimensions of the frame are equal to the final dimensions of the intarsia project. Cut a ¼"-deep by ¼"-wide dado (groove) ⅛" from the back on the inside edge of all four frame pieces for the backing board.

2

Cut the accent strip groove. You can leave the front of the frame solid, but a contrasting accent strip adds to the appeal of the frame. Cut a ¼"-wide by ⅛"-deep dado down the center of the face of all four frame pieces.

3 **Add the accent strip.** I use black walnut. Cut four ¼"-wide by ⅛"-thick strips. Glue the strip into the groove and sand it flush with the top of the frame. Cut the strips to length. Cut the backing board to size, dry assemble the frame, and check the fit.

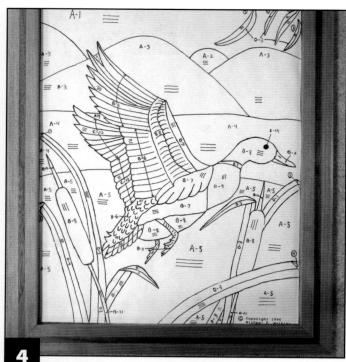

4 **Assemble the frame.** Disassemble the frame and apply glue to the miter joints and in the backing board groove. Reassemble the frame and backing board. Clamp the pieces together until the glue dries. Sand the frame and apply a polyurethane finish. Place a pattern inside the frame for reference.

5 **Assemble the intarsia.** Assemble the cut pieces inside the frame using the pattern as a guide. Remove the top section of the intarsia and pull out the pattern. Apply glue to the back of the top pieces and replace them onto the backing board. Remove, glue, and replace the intarsia pieces, working your way to the bottom.

6 **Finish the project.** Remove any glue squeeze-out. Apply your finish of choice. I apply several coats of satin spray polyurethane. This finish seals the wood and does not reflect light or create a glare. Apply light coats of polyurethane, spraying from all four sides to get even coverage.

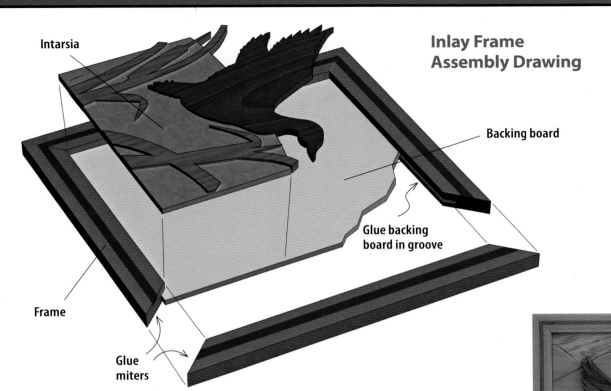

Intarsia

Backing board

Glue backing
board in groove

Frame

Glue
miters

Materials & Tools

INLAY FRAME
Materials:
- 2 each ¾" x 1½" x 16¼" cherry (frame)
- 2 each ¾" x 1½" x 13¼" cherry (frame)
- 2 each ⅛" x ¼" x 12¼" walnut (accent)
- 2 each ⅛" x ¼" x 15⅝" walnut (accent)
- ¼" x 11" x 14" lauan plywood (backer)
- Spray satin polyurethane
- Hanging hook

Tools:
- Router table
- Miter saw or miter box
- Table saw
- Planer to plane wood to proper thickness for inlay
- Square and clamps for frame assembly

MALLARD INTARSIA
Materials:
- ³⁄₁₆" x 3" x 12" tulipwood (A-1)
- ³⁄₁₆" x 2" x 2" pau amarillo (A-2)
- ³⁄₁₆" x 5" x 12" poplar (A-3)
- ³⁄₁₆" x 3½" x 12" ipe (A-4)
- ³⁄₁₆" x 8" x 12" ash (A-5)
- ½" x 2" x 3" pau amarillo (B-2)
- ½" x 2½" x 2½" poplar (B-3)
- ½" x 4" x 8" walnut (B-6)
- ½" x 3" x 6" holly (B-7)
- ½" x 2" x 10" lacewood (B-8)
- ½" x 1½" x 2½" bloodwood (B-9)
- ½" x 1" x 2" mahogany (B-10)
- ½" x 1" x 4" canarywood (B-11)
- ⅜" x 2½" x 3" fishtail oak (C-12)
- ⅜" x 1½" x 3" purpleheart (C-13)
- ⅝" x 5" x 10" poplar (D-3)

- ⅛" x 1" x 1" ebony (E-14)
- Carbon paper, spray adhesive, or 8½" x 11" labels
- Spray satin polyurethane
- Assorted grits of sandpaper
- Wood glue

Tools:
- Scroll saw blades of choice
- Rotary power carver with ⁵⁄₆₄"-diameter high speed cutter and ½"-diameter sanding drum
- Belt sander

Note: Mike Mathieu has a detailed labeling system that uses letters to indicate thickness and numbers to indicate species of wood.

Use this custom frame to display photographs, fretwork portraits, woodburnings, or other artwork.

SPECIAL SOURCES

A 60-piece kit for the mallard project, including 15 woods, is available at www.midlothianwoodworks.com.

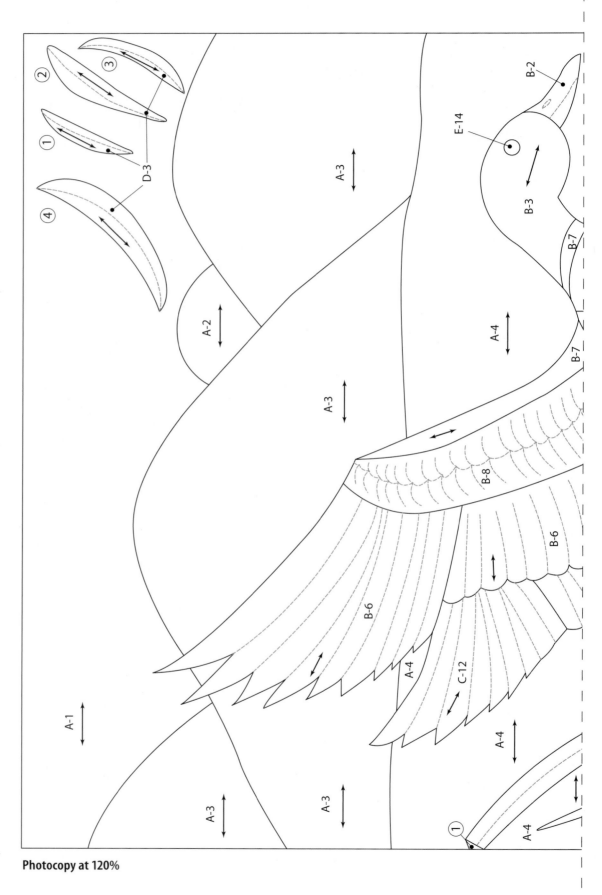

Photocopy at 120%

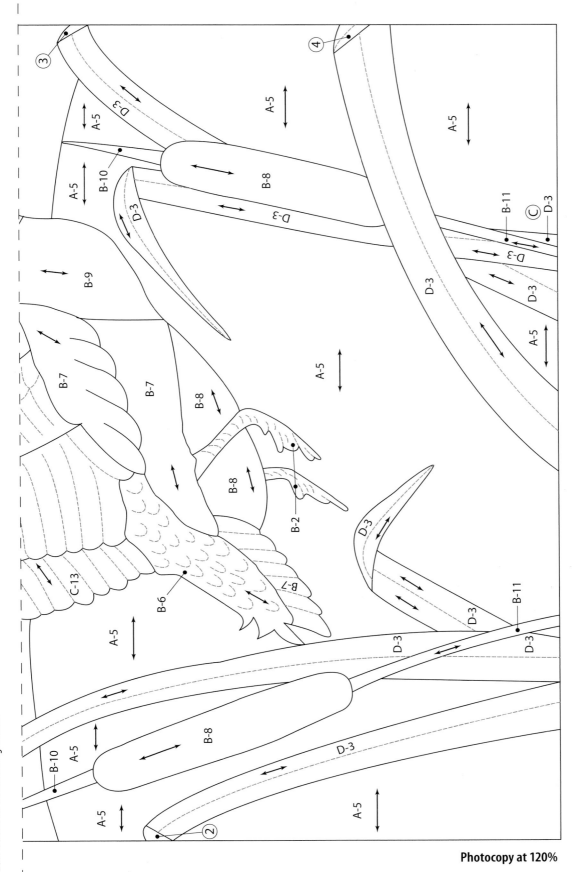

Recess E-14 (eye) into B-3 with a moto tool. Cut the overlapping leaves (1-4) to fit over the edge of the frame.

Photocopy at 120%

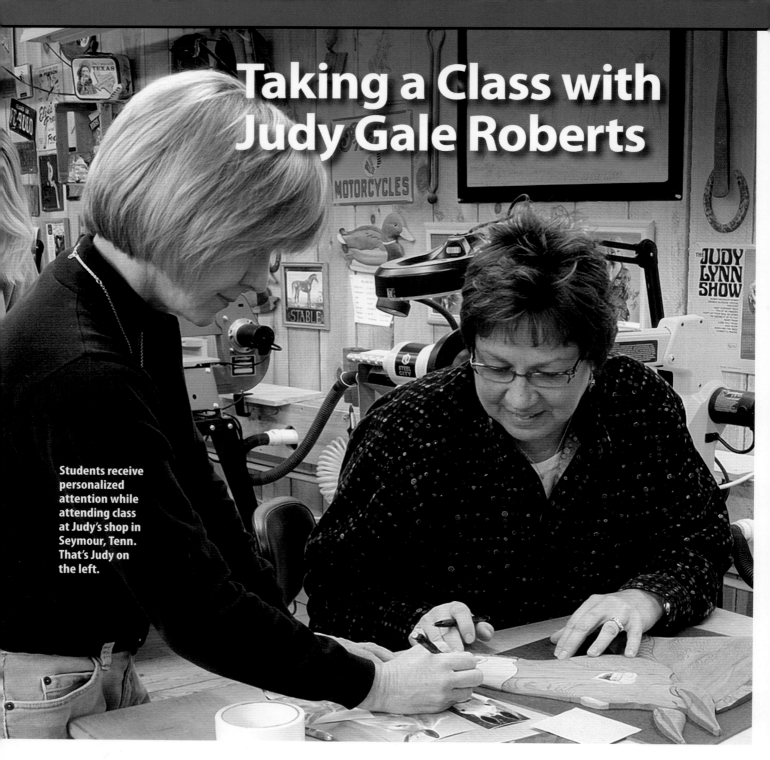

Taking a Class with Judy Gale Roberts

Students receive personalized attention while attending class at Judy's shop in Seymour, Tenn. That's Judy on the left.

Many people credit Judy Gale Roberts with reintroducing the art of intarsia to the public. Judy has devoted her life to creating intarsia designs and teaching others how to create intarsia masterpieces. She was one of the first ten people inducted into the Woodworking Hall of Fame because of her passion for teaching, designing, and creating intarsia.

In addition to creating intarsia patterns, Judy maintains an intense teaching schedule at her home studio in Seymour, Tenn. Speaking from her studio, Judy shares her wisdom by answering some of the questions most commonly asked by students in her intarsia classes.

Q. What kind of wood is best for intarsia?

A. Any species of wood will work. The color and grain configuration are the key factors in creating beautiful intarsia pieces. It is a good idea to have a combination of wood with straight grain along with more figured wood. About 90% of the wood I use is western red cedar, because it is lightweight, easy to work with, and comes in a variety of colors and figures. I use basswood for flesh tones, aspen for the lightest shades, and walnut for the darkest shades. I also use yellowheart and redheart on some of my projects.

Most projects require at least four different shades of wood. This photo shows the variety of colors you can find in western red cedar.

Intarsia requires a combination of highly figured and straight-grained wood. Both of these characteristics can be found in western red cedar, as illustrated above.

Q. How many shades of wood do you need?

A. I recommend at least four shades of wood for most projects. Of course, more variety is better. I like boards that vary in color from edge to edge. Boards that have lighter sapwood on one edge and gradually get darker across the board are great for shading.

Q. What is the best thickness of wood to use?

A. I use ¾"-thick wood for nearly all of my projects. For more dimension, you can use thicker wood, but it is much harder to cut the parts square. The larger the project, the thicker the wood should be—otherwise, it will look flat. To add more depth, I'll often cut shims from plywood or scrap wood and insert them under some of the interior pieces.

Q. What size scroll saw blade do you use?

A. I use a #5 reverse skip-tooth blade for most of the intarsia pieces. The midrange size makes it easier to keep the blade cutting square. If I cut a large part into smaller parts that will go back together, I use a smaller blade. The smaller kerf helps the pieces fit together better. There are many different saw blades, and it is best to have a variety to choose from. From board to board, even within the same species, you may need to try different blades. What works on one piece of wood may not work well on a different piece.

Judy uses a #5 reverse skip-tooth blade. Reverse-tooth blades have teeth pointed in the opposite direction on the bottom, which produce cleaner cuts.

The shim (piece R) will lift the pieces forming the face, giving the illusion of thicker wood.

Q. Why don't my pieces fit together? Will cutting outside the line or re-marking pattern lines improve the fit?

A. Check to make sure your blade is square to the table of your saw. If the table and blade are square, check your cut parts with a square. If the sawn edge of a part isn't square with its flat face, you may be pushing too hard or trying to cut too fast. This happens more often when you cut a curve than it does when cutting straight parts. It is easy to apply pressure from the side to keep the blade on the line, which causes the blade to bend.

I do not recommend cutting heavy and sanding to the line. Most sanders do not sand square to the table. It may look like the parts fit on the surface, but when you start sanding the wood to various thicknesses, gaps will start to appear. This method usually requires more time trying to make the parts fit.

Nor do I recommend cutting a part and re-marking adjoining parts on the pattern. Occasionally, if a part is cut off a little, you can re-mark the adjoining part on the pattern. However, if you do this to each part and your placement is slightly off, the cumulative effect could be a disaster. If your project has 10 or fewer parts, you may be able to get away with it.

Q. What kind of sander works best for contouring intarsia pieces? What diameter drums and grits of sandpaper do you use on the sanders?

A. I equip my grinders with a variety of sanders. I have two pneumatic drum (inflatable) sanders, a flexible-drum sander that has a foam core, and some small inflatable sanders I use for detailing.

The pneumatic drum and flexible-drum sanders make it easy to contour the wood. I have an 8"-diameter by 9"-wide and a 2"-diameter by 8"-wide pneumatic sanding drum. On the larger drum I have a 100-grit sanding sleeve and the smaller drum has a 180-grit sleeve. The flexible-drum sander is 2½" in diameter by 7" wide.

I use the largest diameter drum to rough in the parts and remove wood quickly. The smaller drum removes the scratches from the larger drum. The smaller the diameter of the sander, the harder it is to make a smooth consistent contour. The flexible-drum sander is the smallest I use when sanding intarsia, especially when rough shaping the parts.

The small inflatable sanders are ¾"-diameter by 1"-wide and 1⅝"-diameter by 1¾"-wide. These sanders are used for detailing and sanding hard-to-reach areas. I have an 80-grit sleeve on the very smallest sander and a 220-grit sleeve on the larger one. After all of the parts are roughed in, I remove the cross-grain sanding marks with the larger sanders, and then I go over the surface using the 220-grit sleeve.

Judy uses an 8"-diameter drum with a 100-grit sanding sleeve to remove wood quickly.

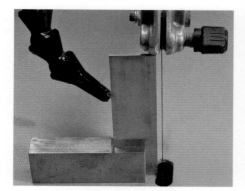

Your blade must be square to your saw table to produce close-fitting intarsia.

Q. Where do I start sanding?

A. This is probably the number one question students ask. Take your time and study the project before beginning. Use reference photos of your subject matter to guide you. Once you sand the wood down, you can't put it back.

Do not start at one end and work your way to the other. Instead, think of the project in layers and start on the background elements or the lowest parts of the project. You need to have at least three thicknesses of wood to give your project dimension. Sand as much as you can off of the background parts to give you more freedom when shaping the foreground sections. Don't just round the edges, but work to reduce the thickness of the entire piece. Rough in the entire project, focusing on the dimensional aspect, before adding details.

Just because the color changes does not mean the contour changes. I use sanding shims or backers to shape multiple parts as a unit. To create a sanding shim, cut scrap wood or plywood to the size of the parts you want to sand as a unit. Use light-duty double-sided carpet tape to hold the parts onto the shim as you shape them.

The arrows (left) show a piece that has been sanded too thin. Cut a shim to fit under the piece (right), raising the piece to the correct height.

Q. I sanded off too much wood. Is there anything I can do now?

A. If the pieces that are too thin are interior parts, you can cut shims to raise them. If it is an exterior part, it is more difficult. You may be able to sand the parts around it thinner, but it is probably easier to re-cut the part. You can spend an hour trying to make it work when it may only take 10 minutes to re-cut the part. The only other option would be to make a shim out of the same wood you are raising. Match up the grain on the outside edges to make it less noticeable.

Q. Do you glue the parts to a backing board or edge glue the parts together?

A. I use a backing board on all of my intarsia projects. This ensures your project will stay together for many years to come. Using a backing board also allows the wood to expand and contract with the humidity. Edge gluing can put the wood in a bind and cause parts to crack when the weather changes. I do edge glue some small parts together, such as the parts of an eye.

Use sanding shims for areas that should be shaped as a unit, such as the spots on this dog.

Seasonal Accents

Every season has its highlights, and this chapter gathers a wealth of them.

Thinking spring? Take a look at the bunny, blossom, rose, and Communion projects.

If summer is on your mind, check out the magnolia door topper, seaside scene, sunflower wreath, and lighthouse.

For fall, there's a scarecrow, a turkey, and a picture frame made of vibrant leaves. And come winter, you can't go wrong with the cardinal photo frame or birds and berries wreath.

Now you just have to decide which one to do first!

Seaside Serenity, by Judy Gale Roberts, page 51.

Judy Gale Roberts 2010

Spring Bunnies

By Frank Droege

This colorful scene of spring is an example of mosaic segmentation. You'll end up with a piece that projects a look of intarsia but with a flat surface, and the numerous colors are from paints, not different colored woods.

Rounding the corners will give the finished artwork the illusion of a ceramic tile. This project can hang as a plaque, but if the loose pieces are not glued, you can give your child a puzzle.

Begin this project by making multiple copies of the pattern while retaining the original one. Remember, you can simplify the project by removing lines and decreasing the number of pieces in any pattern.

Step 1: Prepare the blank. Start by cutting out a piece of wood a little larger than the pattern you wish to scroll. Number each piece of the pattern. Make an extra copy of the marked pattern for reference. Glue the pattern onto the board.

Step 2: Using the #2 reverse-tooth blade, first saw the frame and then the remaining pieces.

Step 3: Remove the burrs from the backs of the pieces with 220-grit sandpaper.

Step 4: Transfer the numbers to the bottom of each piece. Then carefully pull the paper pattern off the wood.

Step 5: Sand the project. Start by dry assembling the pieces inside the frame and sand them with the 220-grit

sandpaper. Then round over the edges of the pieces with the handheld grinder. Leave the outer edge of the frame square.

Step 6: Paint the project. Use a tack cloth to remove any sawdust from the pieces. Then, using the acrylic paint of your choice, paint the sides and edges of each piece according to your color plan.

Step 7: Glue the frame to the backing. Starting with a corner piece, carefully assemble and glue the pieces in the frame with yellow wood glue. Add any fine details, such as eyes, with paint or a woodburner.

Step 8: When the glue has dried, according to the manufacturer's directions, apply a satin varnish to the entire piece. Then hang the piece for display with sawtooth hooks or wire and eye hooks.

Materials & Tools

Materials:
- ⅜" x 13½" x 10¼" white pine or white cedar or softwood of choice (pattern board)
- ⅛" x 13½" x 10¼" (backer board)
- Temporary bond spray adhesive
- Sandpaper, 220 grit
- Acrylic craft paints of choice
- Yellow wood glue
- Acrylic varnish
- Sawtooth hooks or wire and eye hooks

Tools:
- #2 reverse-tooth blade
- Handheld grinder or micro motor tool with ¼" sand band, for smooth edges
- Woodburner (optional)

Photocopy at 145%

Blossoms

By Frank Droege

Like most of my mosaics, these use scroll saw cuts
to separate and accent details. Painting the segments
before assembly makes finishing quick and easy. I use
acrylic paints, but the project would also look nice with
wood stains or dyes. This design can be used as a wall
hanging or trivet.

Photocopy at 100%

Rose

By Frank Droege

Roses are a symbol of love and beauty. This single bud can be displayed alone, and also looks great when grouped with similar segmentation projects, such as the blossoms design. I like to work with segmentation because the individual pieces make it easy to achieve a perfect finish.

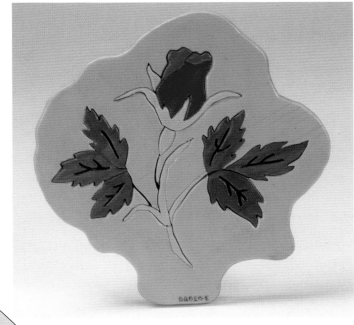

Photocopy at 100%

Classic Cup and Loaf Intarsia

By Dennis Simmons

This classic cup and loaf intarsia, which looks good with or without the cross, is a perfect introduction to the art form. If this is your first intarsia project, you may want to make it once without the cross, then expand your skill set the second time you make it by adding the cross insert.

I used aromatic red cedar for the cup, pine for the side of the loaf, aspen for the front, and cherry for the crust, with the cross of any contrasting wood. However, this project can be made with a variety of wood types and color combinations, so this is a good time to use scrap pieces and create an attractive project without a large investment in expensive woods. All the wood pieces start at ¾" thick.

Start by cutting the pattern into separate pieces, using a razor knife. Where pieces join, be as accurate as possible. Leave extra paper around the edges of the pattern with no adjoining pieces. This helps to distinguish areas where accurate cutting is needed and where accuracy is less important. I use a glue stick to apply glue to the back of the pattern pieces and attach them to the wood.

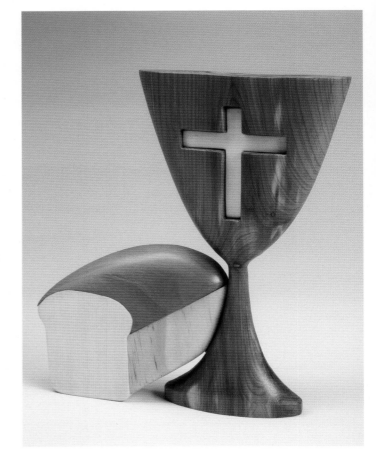

TIP **QUICK CLAMPS FOR SMALL GLUE-UPS**

Fill a large pill bottle with weight for an inexpensive clamp.

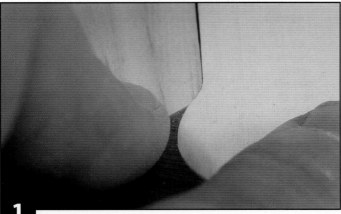

1 **Cut out the pieces.** Using a #5 reverse skip-tooth blade, cut slowly; accuracy is more important than speed, and it takes less time to cut the pieces accurately the first time. Inaccuracy leads to repair work, more cutting, and fitting. Test fit the pieces together. Gaps like those shown in the photo are the result of inaccurate cutting. Hold the pieces together and cut the points of contact. Make multiple cuts with the scroll saw blade, passing between the pieces until a suitable fit is attained.

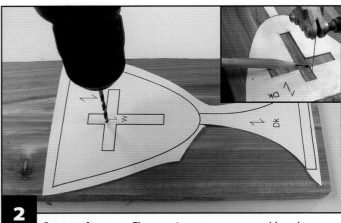

2 **Cut out the cross.** The cross insert presents a problem, because it is an inside piece that must be cut precisely the same size and shape as the piece being removed. It is important to make sure your blade is square before cutting the cross. Drill a blade-entry hole, insert the scroll saw blade, and cut around the perimeter of the cross. Be sure to remove it in one piece.

3 **Use the cross cutout as a guide for the cross insert.** Glue the cutout top-side down to ¼"-thick wood of a contrasting color. Orienting the grain of the contrasting wood at 90° to the cutout will strengthen the cross. I use wood glue and clamp the cross using a pill bottle filled with weight. When it is dry, carefully cut out the cross. The laminated cross piece should fit into the original cup. Glue the cross in place. Use a wood chisel to trim the extra thickness off the bottom side of the cross.

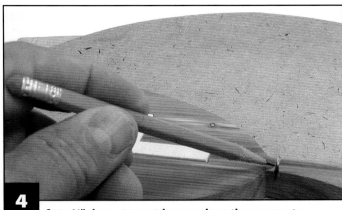

4 **Cut a ¼"-deep stop notch near where the cup meets the stem.** This notch represents the lowest point in the project. All carving will be done from each end and will stop at the notch.

5 **Shape the cup.** Use double-sided carpet tape to attach the back of the cup to the workbench. I use a sharp wood chisel as a carving tool to remove unwanted wood, because it keeps sanding to a minimum. However, you could also do all of the shaping by sanding. If you use the chisel, remember that keeping it at a low angle removes less wood; a higher angle removes more wood.

6 **Shape the foot and stem.** Shape the foot end by rounding the corners with a carving chisel until it curves smoothly, with no flat area in the center of the board. Use the chisel to shape the stem area, cutting from the foot toward the stop notch. The center of the stem at the notch should be approximately ⅜" thick. Round over the edges of the stem, but leave a flat area approximately ¼" thick (pointed out by the pencil line) where the bread will adjoin the stem.

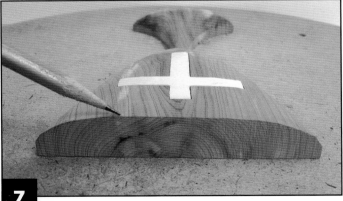

7 **Round off the edges of the cup.** A flat area may remain near the center. Round the area near the notch to blend in with the stem.

Materials & Tools

Materials:
- ¾" x 5" x 8" red cedar
- ¾" x 3" x 3" aspen
- ¾" x 3" x 3" pine
- ¾" x 3" x 5" cherry
- ⅛" x 7" x 8" plywood
- Glue stick
- Wood glue
- Cyanoacrylate glue
- Carpet tape
- Sandpaper, 100, 150, & 220 grits
- Craft sticks with sandpaper attached to them
- ½"-diameter dowel rod with sandpaper attached to it

- Polyurethane finish of choice

Tools:
- Razor knife
- Small square
- #5 reverse skip-tooth blades or blades of choice
- ¾"-wide wood chisel
- Drill with ⅛"-diameter bit
- Small paintbrush
- Pill bottle filled with pebbles (to use as a clamping weight)

8 **Shape the bread.** The front piece of the loaf stays at ¾" thick, but the side and crust must taper smoothly down to meet the cup. Taper the side from ¾" where it contacts the front to ¼" where it meets the cup. Taper the crust from ¾" where it meets the front to ⅜" to coincide with the side. Round the edge of the crust to match the thickness of the side, and round over the top of the crust all along the top edge.

9 **Sand and finish.** Use 100-grit sandpaper to remove the chisel marks. Blend the rounded areas with the craft stick or dowel sanding tools. Remove any sanding marks with 150- to 180-grit sandpaper. Apply two coats of wipe-on polyurethane finish with a small brush, dipping it just enough to wet the surface. Coat the edges first, then lay the piece on cardboard to coat the face. Avoid getting finish on the back. When it's dry, sand with 220-grit sandpaper before applying a second coat.

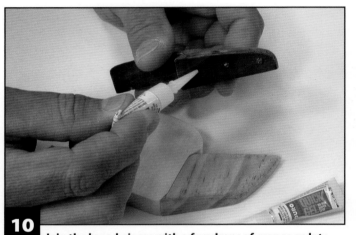

10 **Join the bread pieces with a few drops of cyanoacrylate (CA) glue.** Apply several drops to the edges of the pieces, then hold them together on a flat surface for 15 to 20 seconds. This just makes it easier to position all the pieces on the backer board.

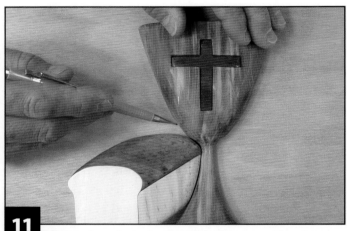

11 **Mark and cut the backer board.** Hold the cup and bread pieces together and trace the outline onto ⅛"-thick plywood backer board with a pencil. Cut out the backer board following the pencil lines.

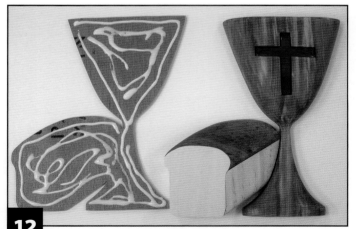

12 **Glue the pieces to the backing board.** Put wood glue on the backing board, then align the cup and loaf pieces. Use the pill bottle weight to clamp them until the glue has dried. You can sand and finish the back and edges of the backing board, if you wish.

TIP   **A SQUARE TABLE**

Use a small metal square and a wood block covered with white paper to make sure your blade is square to your table. The wood block makes it easier to see the saw blade and the square. Place the block behind the saw blade, and check table and blade angle. Adjust table to attain a parallel gap between the blade and the square.

By choosing different hardwoods and finishes, you can achieve a variety of artistic effects to the completed project.

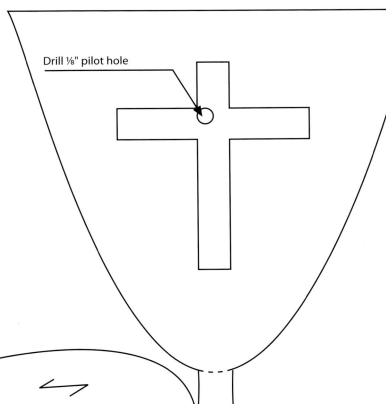

Drill ⅛" pilot hole

Cherry or walnut

Pine, medium brown

Aspen or other white wood

Red cedar

Photocopy at 100%

Creating a Magnolia Door Topper

By Judy Gale Roberts

This beautiful door topper is the perfect way to celebrate spring. While the graceful floral design is a welcome addition year round, a convenient hanger allows you to change the door topper with each season.

To simplify the pattern, eliminate the frame. Select a nice piece of plywood for the backing board, which doubles as the background of the design.

Wood Selection

This project requires four different shades of wood. Western red cedar is an excellent choice because it comes in a variety of shades. You can often find several shades in the same board. Substitute walnut if you can't find dark western red cedar. Western red cedar is found more often at lumber yards than home improvement centers or specialty wood stores. The wood is commonly used for fence material and siding because it resists decay and bugs.

Cutting the Pieces

Make at least five copies of the pattern. Keep one copy as a master pattern. Cut apart each piece of the pattern that has a different color or grain direction. If the color and grain direction are the same, such as the leaf areas, you can keep these sections together.

Cut your patterns about ¼" outside the lines. Use repositionable spray adhesive or a re-stickable glue stick to attach the patterns to the wood.

I use #5 and #0 skip reverse-tooth blades. The reversed teeth on the bottom of the blade reduce the fuzzies on the bottom of the piece. Use the smaller blade to cut interior lines, such as the lines down the center of each leaf. Stop often and sand away any fuzzies on the back of the blank.

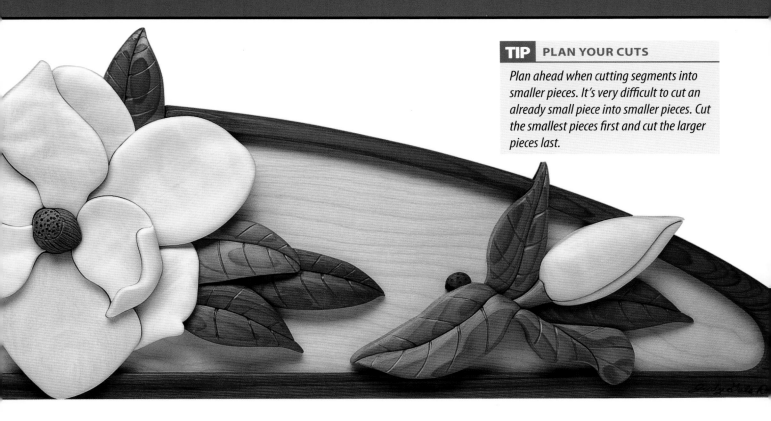

TIP | **PLAN YOUR CUTS**

Plan ahead when cutting segments into smaller pieces. It's very difficult to cut an already small piece into smaller pieces. Cut the smallest pieces first and cut the larger pieces last.

These little bits of wood can change the cutting angle causing a poor fit. Use a small square to make sure the saw blade remains square to the saw table.

Experiment to determine what saw speed gives you the greatest control. Use a lighted magnifier and a foot switch to make it easier to cut accurately.

Sanding the Project

I use a soft flexible-drum sander, which makes it easier to get soft contours. The sander is also soft on the end, making carving with the sander a possibility. Remove most of the material with 80-grit sandpaper and then smooth it out with 120-grit sandpaper.

1 **Cut the pieces and check the fit.** Cut the large blanks into manageable pieces about the size of your hand. Warm up by cutting the easy parts first. Sand any burrs off of the bottom and write the piece number on the back. Dry assemble the project and check the fit. If the pieces do not fit together, use a sharp blade to trim any areas where the pattern line remains. Do not sand the sides. If necessary, cut a new piece. Remove the patterns.

2 **Determine your sanding plan.** Sand each element to the appropriate depth before shaping the pieces. Always remove the wood from the top of the piece. Create a few sanding shims to shape the leaves as units. The same shim can be re-used for additional leaves. Attach the leaf parts to the shims with double-sided tape. Use ¼"-thick plywood to create risers for the parts marked R on the pattern.

MAGNOLIA: ESTABLISHING LEVELS

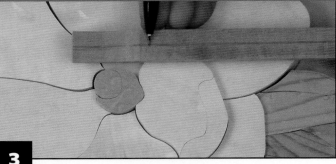

3 **Sand the frame.** The frame is thinner than the intarsia to give the appearance of the leaves and blooms overlapping the frame. If you did not cut the frame pieces from ⅜"-thick wood, sand the frame pieces down to ⅜" thick. Draw a line along the edge of the frame pieces as a guide. Mark the height of adjoining frame pieces on the leaves and blooms with a pencil.

4 **Sand the lowest leaves.** Start with the leaf at the top of the magnolia bloom. Taper the leaf down toward the flower petal. Do not sand below the pencil lines indicating the frame. Sketch a guideline on the edges of the leaves. Sand the two leaves that tuck under the magnolia buds down to ⅜" thick and taper them down to ¼" thick where they join the bud and stem.

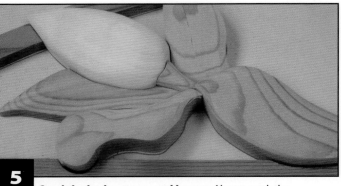

5 **Sand the buds, stems, and leaves.** Always mark the thickness of adjoining pieces before sanding the next piece. Sand the remaining leaves. Keep the leaves on top of other leaves thicker. Sand the stems down to ⅝" thick. Taper the stem where it joins the leaves and round the sides. Create a sanding shim for the bud and round the sides of both buds. Do not sand below the line showing where the bud joins the frame.

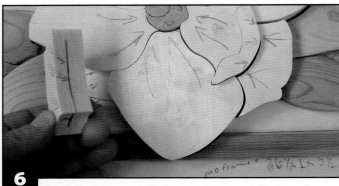

6 **Sand the lower petals.** Taper each outer petal in toward the center of the flower. Stay above the pencil lines showing the thickness of the leaves. The outside petals are farther away from the viewer and should be thinner than the petals touching the flower center. The flower center and the petal just to the right of the center are elevated by a rising shim.

MAGNOLIA: ADDING THE DETAILS

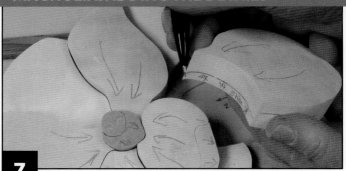

7 **Continue shaping the petals.** Mark the thickness of the riser on the adjoining petals. Do not sand below the riser line. Taper the petals touching the center as you did with the outer petals, but keep the center petals thicker. The petals curl up around the outer edges. Press the center of each petal firmly against the soft edges of the flexible-drum sander and drag the petal across the edge of the sander.

8 **Add curves and details to the petals.** Use reference photos to help you create realistic contours and details on the petals and leaves. Sketch in the curves before shaping them with the sander. Add the curves and details to the petals using the edge of the flexible-drum sander.

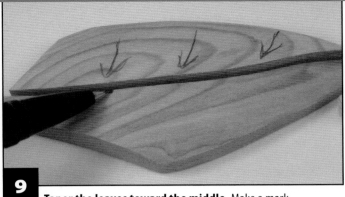

9 **Taper the leaves toward the middle.** Make a mark ⅛" down from the top on the center of one leaf segment. Taper the leaf in toward the center, down to the pencil line. Place the shaped segment beside the second leaf segment. Draw a guideline along the contour and taper the second segment to the line.

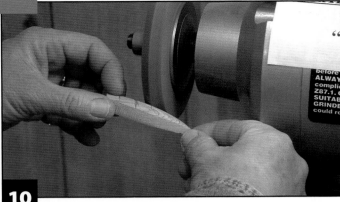

10 **Add the leaf veins.** Use the pattern as a guide to sketch the veins on the leaves at a 45° angle. I dress the edge of a Wonder Wheel to a V-shape and use the wheel to carve and burnish the leaf veins in one step. You can also use a woodburner or rotary power carver to add the vein lines.

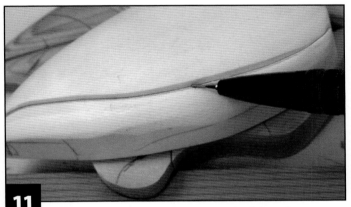

11 **Detail the magnolia buds.** Make a mark ⅛" down from the top of the smaller section and sand down to this line. This provides separation between the bud's petals. Use the smaller section to draw a guideline on the bigger petal and gently round the edge of the petal, staying above the guideline.

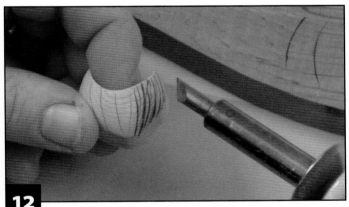

12 **Woodburn the flower center.** Woodburn the lines around the center circle with a chisel-tip woodburning tip. Use a round tip to burn in the dot texture in the center of the blossom. Practice on scrap wood before burning the textures on your project.

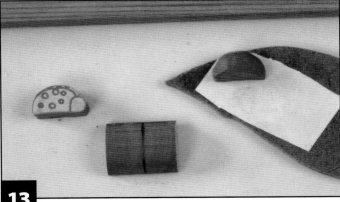

13 **Cut and sand the ladybugs.** Transfer the pattern to ¾"-thick redheart and cut out as many ladybugs as you'd like. Cut the ¾"-thick blank in half to produce a left- and right-facing ladybug. Attach the ladybugs to a piece of hardboard with double-sided tape to sand and shape the small pieces.

14 **Add the ladybug details.** Use the pattern as a guide to draw the head and wing line. Use the chisel point of the woodburner to burn in the lines and shade the head. Use the round-point woodburner tip to add the spots. The ladybug is cut on a curve, so it will sit on any of the curved lines.

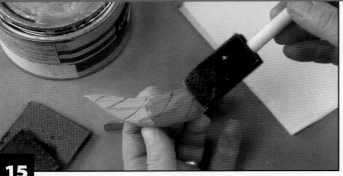

15 **Apply the finish.** Apply a heavy coat of polyurethane wiping gel to each piece with a 1"-wide disposable foam brush. Wait 45 seconds and then wipe off the excess finish with a paper towel. Buff the piece with a clean paper towel. Let the finish dry for 6 to 8 hours and apply a second lighter coat using the same technique. Check any white wood for raised grain and smooth if necessary with fine steel wool. Apply a third coat of finish.

16 **Cut the backing board.** Attach a pattern to the plywood with spray adhesive. You may need to use spiral blades or cut the backing board with a saber saw. Cut ¹⁄₁₆" inside the exterior lines of the pattern. To keep the finish from the areas to be glued, cut the paper pattern ⅛" inside the intarsia elements with a hobby knife. Peel off the pattern between these elements. Seal and finish the exposed plywood with a clear acrylic spray finish. Stain the edges of the backing board with dark stain.

17 **Glue the intarsia to the backing board.** Check the placement of the intarsia on the backing board, remove the patterns, and use small amounts of yellow wood glue to attach the intarsia to the backing board. While gluing, use hot glue to lock a few pieces in place if desired. Use a straight edge, such as a level, to ensure the bottom edge of the door topper is straight.

18 **Attach the hanger to the back of the project.** Hold the project with your thumb and middle finger and move it back and forth until the project balances. Mark that location and pre-drill the hole for the hanger screw with a bit slightly smaller than the screw. Try to position the hanger in a section where the wood is thicker. Attach the hanger with the appropriate screw.

Materials & Tools

Materials:

- ¾" x 5½" x 9½" medium-dark wood, such as western red cedar, mahogany, or American beech (leaves)
- ⅜" to ¾" x 5½" x 36½" medium-dark wood, such as western red cedar, mahogany, or American beech (frame)
- ¾" x 5½" x 21" medium shade of wood, such as a western red cedar, aromatic cedar, cherry, or red oak (leaves and stems)
- ¾" x 2" x 3" light wood, such as western red cedar, cypress, or white oak (flower center)
- ¾" x 5½" x 22" white wood, such as aspen, basswood, white pine, holly, or poplar (flowers)
- ⅛" to ¼" x 5½" x 36½" maple or light-colored plywood (backing board)
- ¾" x 2" x 2" redheart (ladybugs)
- Assorted scraps of Baltic birch plywood (sanding shims and risers)
- Repositionable spray adhesive or re-stickable glue stick
- 5 photocopies of the pattern

- Yellow wood glue
- Double-sided light-duty carpet tape
- Polyurethane wiping gel or finish of choice
- Paper towels
- 1"-wide disposable foam brush
- Mirror hanger with #6 by ½"-long sheet metal screw or hanger of choice

Tools:

- #5 and #0 skip reverse-tooth blades or blades of choice
- Sander of choice (I use a flexible-drum sander)
- Woodburner with chisel and round tips
- Carving or hobby knife (to cut pattern on backing board)
- Saber saw or spiral blades (to cut backing board)
- Wonder Wheel or rotary power carver (optional) —see page 140
- Drill with drill bit slightly smaller than hanger screw

I used some redheart wood for the ladybugs. If you make the ladybugs, it is easier to shape and add detail if you leave it the full thickness. Once it is the desired shape and the spots are burned in, then turn it on the side and slice off the top section. Mine are about ¼" thick. The curve along the lower edge of the ladybug makes it easy to place on the sides of any leaf or petal.

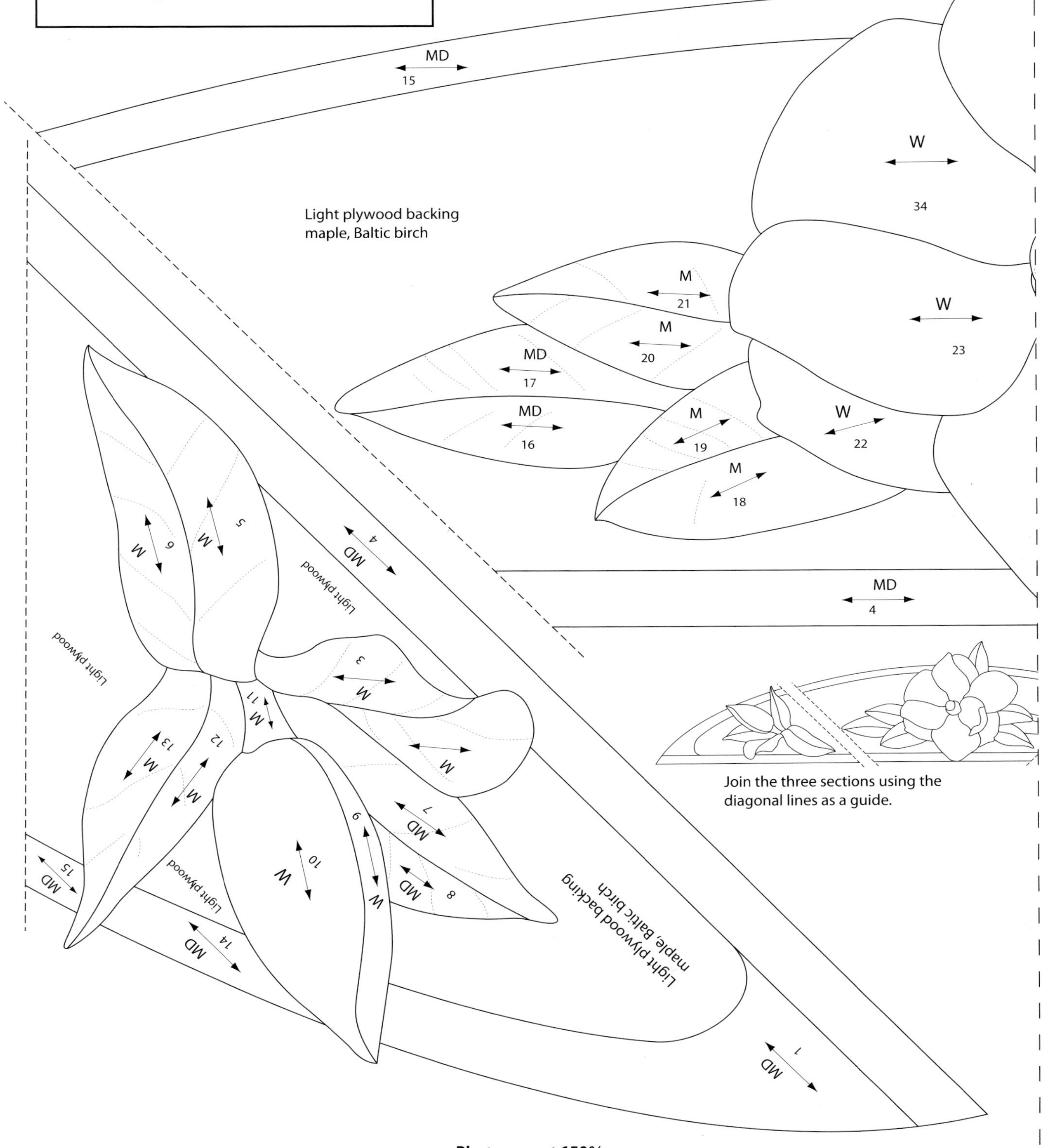

MD
15

W
34

Light plywood backing
maple, Baltic birch

M
21

W
23

M
20

MD
17

M
19

W
22

MD
16

M
18

Light plywood

Light plywood

MD
4

6
M

5
M

MD
4

MD
4

3
M

11
M

13
M

12

M

MD
15

MD
14

10
W

9
W

7
MD

8
MD

1
MD

Light plywood

Light plywood backing
maple, Baltic birch

Join the three sections using the
diagonal lines as a guide.

Photocopy at 150%

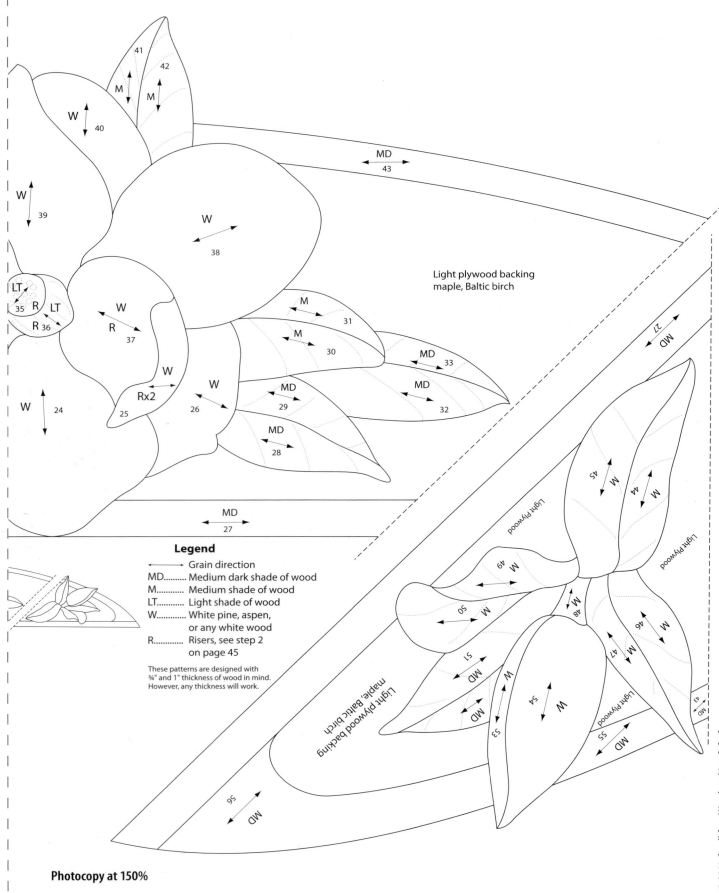

Legend

⟵⟶ Grain direction
MD.......... Medium dark shade of wood
M............ Medium shade of wood
LT........... Light shade of wood
W............ White pine, aspen,
   or any white wood
R............. Risers, see step 2
   on page 45

These patterns are designed with
¾" and 1" thickness of wood in mind.
However, any thickness will work.

Light plywood backing
maple, Baltic birch

Photocopy at 150%

Seaside Serenity

By Judy Gale Roberts

This relaxing beach scene is a great way to celebrate summer. The peaceful portrait serves as a snapshot of those lazy days on the shore in the warm sun.

Nearly all of the pieces in this project can be cut from western red cedar fence pickets. The fence pickets are usually 5½" wide by 6' long. Western red cedar comes in a variety of shades and can be found in lumber yards. The wood is commonly used for fence material and siding because it resists decay and bugs.

Make at least five copies of the pattern. When cutting the pattern into pieces, cut about ¼" outside the lines to provide better adhesion to the wood.

Cutting the Pieces

Cut the larger sections into pieces about the size of your hand for easier handling. Remove any tearout or burrs on the bottom of the sections with sandpaper so the pieces sit flat on the saw table.

Use a #5 skip reverse-tooth blade to cut most of the pieces. For a better fit, switch to a #0 skip reverse-tooth blade to cut the interior lines and to separate the pieces with the same grain direction and color.

Accuracy is key. Experiment with the speed of your saw. I run my saw between 60% and 70% of the maximum speed. Align the center of the blade with the center of the line so your cut removes the line.

Stop often to remove any tearout from the back of the pieces. Check cut pieces to make sure your blade is still square with the saw table. Plan your cuts so you can cut small parts free from a larger block.

When all of the parts have been cut, remove any tear out from the back of the pieces. Assemble the pieces and check the fit. Do not sand the sides of the pieces. Use a new sharp blade to trim pieces if necessary. Write the number from the pattern on the back of the piece and remove the patterns.

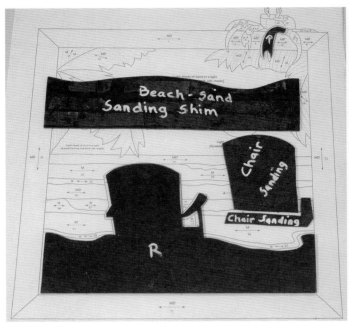

Use sanding shims to shape pieces in sections.
Use rising shims to add dimension to the project.

Sanding and Shaping the pieces

I use a soft flexible-drum sander and two pneumatic-drum sanders to shape the pieces. I remove most of the wood with an 80-grit sanding drum. I smooth out the pieces with a 120-grit sanding drum and finish sand with a 220-grit sanding drum.

Rough in the levels of the entire project before shaping details. Start by lowering the background and parts that would be the farthest from the viewer. Cut pieces of scrap plywood or tempered hardboard to the size of the sections to be sanded as a unit. Use light-duty double-sided carpet tape to attach the parts to the sanding shim. I use a sanding shim for the sand area, including the shadow under the chair. Some of the chair sections can be sanded as a unit to help ensure the angles match up.

Use rising shims to elevate sections of the project. Cut the shims slightly smaller than the shaded sections on the pattern. Place the rising shims in place under the pieces before you begin shaping the project.

SEASIDE: SHAPING THE WATER

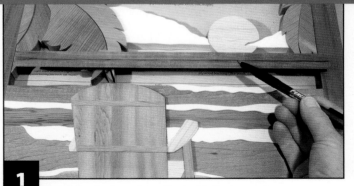

1 **Sand the darker water.** Start with the topmost wave (33), which is farthest from the chair. Sand the piece down to ¼" (6mm) thick and place it back in position. Mark the thickness of this piece on the adjacent pieces (32 and 38). Work toward the sand, sanding each section slightly thicker. The pieces closest to the sand (51, 53, and 56) should be about ½" (13mm) thick.

2 **Lower the wave caps.** Mark the thickness of the surrounding dark water on the white wood and sand the pieces down so they are 1⁄16" (2mm) above the lines. The white wood represents the water bubbling up on the tops of the waves. Do not sand the white waves closest to the beach yet.

3 **Shape the wave caps and mark the sand.** Roll each wave-cap section down along the top edge, leaving it thicker on the bottom edge. Position the last two sections of the dark wave (51 and 56) tightly against the sand and mark the thickness of the waves on the sand. The angle of the sand must match the angle on the waves so the wave appears to be washing up on the shore.

4 **Attach the beach pieces to a sanding shim.** Turn the beach and chair shadow sections upside down and remove any dust or burrs from the back. Cut double-sided tape into 1" (25mm)-wide sections and apply the tape to the back of the pieces. Remove the paper from the tape and attach the sanding shim. Turn the pieces right-side up and press the pieces down on the tape.

SEASIDE: SHAPING THE BEACH & CHAIR

5 **Sand and shape the beach.** Taper the beach section so it is thicker where it meets the frame and tapers down to meet the water's edge. Then sand some dips in the beach with a soft-edge sander for a slightly textured look. Remove the pieces from the shim and place them in position. Sand the white foam of the wave washing up on shore. These pieces are thicker than the surrounding sand.

6 **Attach the chair pieces to the sanding shims.** Mark the thickness of the sand on the chair parts. The legs (60, 62, and 66) taper down 1/16" (2mm) where they meet the chair. Mark the thickness of the legs on the chair. Attach double-sided tape to the L-shaped chair seat and the wide sections of the chair back. Do not apply tape to the thin sections of the chair back. Attach the chair back and seat to separate sanding shims.

7 **Shape the chair.** Taper the small section of the seat (54) down toward the water. Taper the right side of the chair seat down to create the correct angle. Mark where the seat joins the chair back. Sand the chair back at an angle tapering down toward the seat of the chair. The chair back is slightly thinner than the chair seat. The horizontal parts (37 and 49) are slightly thicker than the chair back.

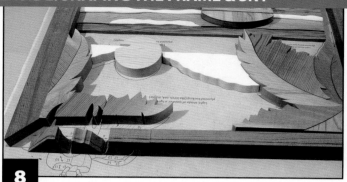

8 Sand the frame. Sand the top frame down to a thickness of ½" (13mm) to give the crab more dimension. Use a sanding shim and sand the top sections as flat as possible. Lightly sand the bottom frame and then taper the sides from the thickness of the bottom frame down to meet the thickness of the top frame.

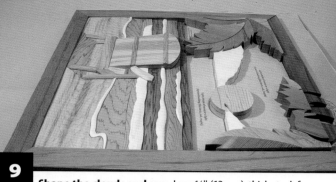

9 Shape the clouds and sun. I use ½" (13mm)-thick stock for the clouds. Shape the larger cloud and mark the thickness on the sun. Sand the sun, leaving it thicker than the large cloud. Mark the thickness of the sun on the smaller cloud and taper the smaller cloud almost down to the sun. Mark the thickness of the clouds on the palm fronds. Keep the fronds thicker than the clouds.

SEASIDE: SHAPING THE FRONDS & CRAB

10 Shape the fronds. Mark the level of the frame on the fronds. The fronds are slightly thinner than the frame. The center ridge is thicker and the outside edges taper down. Start with parts 18 and 19. Parts 20 and 21 are thicker than the first frond. Parts 22 and 23 are thicker than the middle frond, but thinner than the frame. Keep the fronds on the right thinner than the crab and the frame.

11 Shape the crab. Make the back legs (14 and 9) about ⅜" (10mm)-thick. Keep the other legs thicker than the frame, but taper them down to meet the body. Leave the claws (3 and 5) the full thickness. The legs on the left side taper down thinner than the body. Use double-sided tape to attach the body sections (10 and 15) together and shape them as one unit. Angle the bottom section down toward the legs. Round and shape the eyestalks and eyes.

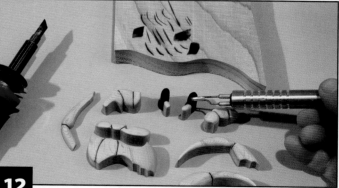

12 Carve and burn in the details. Sand the pieces with 220-grit sandpaper. Use a pencil to mark the detail lines on the chair, palm fronds, and crab. Add the details with a Wonder Wheel dressed to a V-point, carving tools, or a woodburner. The Wonder Wheel carves and burnishes the wood in one stroke. You can cut the eyestalk and eye from one piece of wood and use a woodburner to darken the eye, but it can be difficult to burn the wood evenly.

13 Add highlights to the crab's eyes. Sharpen the ends of a piece of aspen in a pencil sharpener. Drill ⅛" (3mm)-diameter holes in the top part of each eye. Glue the aspen in the holes. When dry, sand the aspen flush with the rest of the eye. Use a small sander and avoid the darker wood to prevent the dark wood dust from staining the aspen. If the aspen does get stained, drill out the aspen and start over.

14 **Apply the finish.** Apply polyurethane wiping gel to the top and sides of each piece with a disposable foam brush. Apply a heavy coat, allow it to dry for less than a minute, and wipe off the excess with a paper towel. Buff the pieces completely dry with a clean paper towel and let them dry for 6 to 8 hours. Apply a lighter coat using the same technique. When dry, rub any areas where the grain raised with fine steel wool and apply a third coat.

15 **Make the backing.** Attach the pattern to clear plywood. Cut 1/16" (2mm) inside the perimeter pattern lines. Use a hobby knife to cut the pattern away from the exposed sky areas. Cut 1/8" (3mm) on the side of the lines that will be covered by the intarsia. The remaining pattern acts as a mask. Apply clear spray acrylic finish to the sky and back of the plywood. Apply dark stain on the edges.

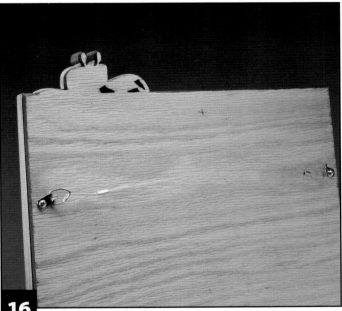

16 **Attach the project.** Place the pieces in position on the backing board. Lift each piece individually and apply a little yellow wood glue to the back. Place the piece back in position. Use hot glue to lock a few key pieces in place. Use a level as a straight edge on the bottom of the project. Attach a mirror hanger or eyelets and wire to the back.

Materials & Tools

Materials:
- ¾" x 5½" x 36½" (20mm x 140mm x 930mm) medium dark wood, such as western red cedar, mahogany, or American beech
- ¾" x 5½" x 20 (20mm x 140mm x 510mm) medium wood, such as western red cedar, aromatic cedar, cherry, or red oak
- ¾" x 5½" x 9" (20mm x 140mm x 230mm) medium light wood, such as western red cedar, maple, or white oak
- ¾" x 5½" x 14" (20mm x 140mm x 355mm) light wood, such as western red cedar, cypress, or white oak
- ⅛" to ¼" x 16" x 18" (3mm to 6mm x 405mm x 460mm) Baltic birch, oak, or maple plywood (backing board)
- ¾" x 5½" x 12" (20mm x 140mm x 305mm) white wood, such as aspen, basswood, white pine, holly, or poplar
- Assorted scraps of ¼" (6mm)-thick tempered hardboard or plywood (rising shims, sanding shims)
- Repositionable spray adhesive or re-stickable glue stick
- 5 photocopies of the pattern
- Yellow wood glue

- Double-sided light-duty carpet tape
- Polyurethane wiping gel or finish of choice
- Paper towels
- 1" (25mm)-wide disposable foam brush
- Mirror hanger or hanger of choice
- Clear acrylic spray finish
- Dark stain (backing board)
- Assorted grits of sanding drums and sandpaper

Tools:
- #5 and #0 reverse skip-tooth blades or blades of choice
- Pneumatic-drum sanders, flexible-drum sanders, or sanders of choice
- Drill with ⅛" (3mm)-diameter bit
- Pencil sharpener
- Woodburner (optional)
- Wonder Wheel or carving knife (optional) —see page 140
- Hobby knife
- Saber saw or circular saw (optional for backer)

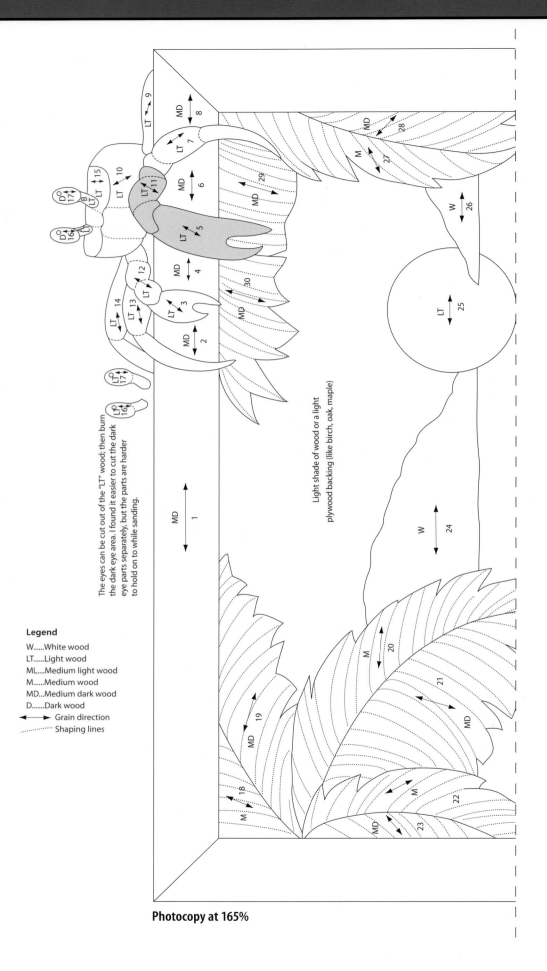

Legend

W......White wood
LT......Light wood
ML....Medium light wood
M......Medium wood
MD...Medium dark wood
D......Dark wood
←——→ Grain direction
······· Shaping lines

The eyes can be cut out of the "LT" wood; then burn the dark eye area. I found it easier to cut the dark eye parts separately, but the parts are harder to hold on to while sanding.

Light shade of wood or a light plywood backing (like birch, oak, maple)

Photocopy at 165%

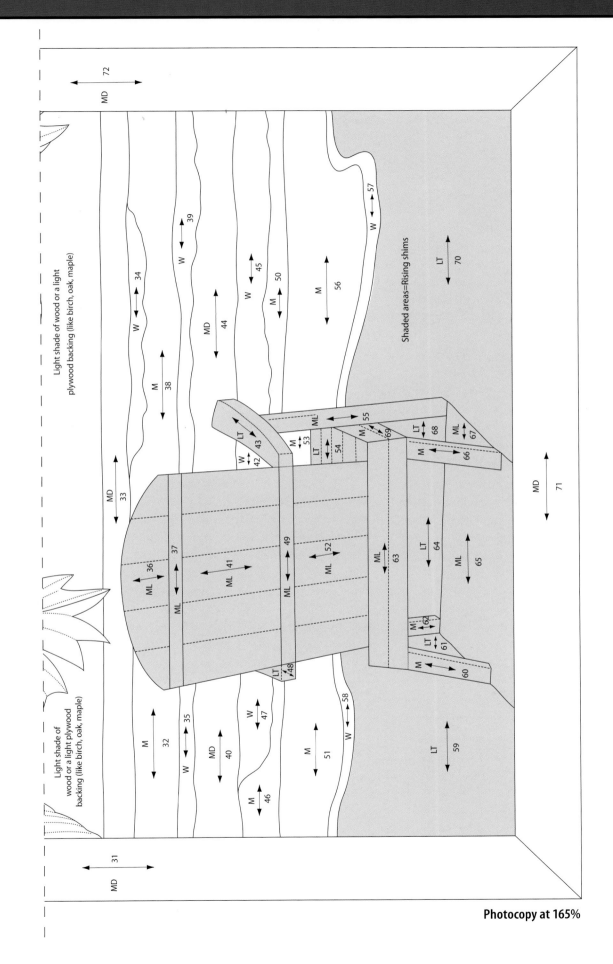

© 2011 Scroll Saw Woodworking & Crafts

Light shade of wood or a light plywood backing (like birch, oak, maple)

Light shade of wood or a light plywood backing (like birch, oak, maple)

Shaded areas=Rising shims

Photocopy at 165%

Summer Sunflower Wreath

By Kathy Wise

The side view shows how the shaping creates dimension.

Sunflowers remind me of carefree days enjoying the summer breeze and crisp white sheets hanging out to dry. For me, they are the perfect symbol of summer. Hang the wreath on your door to share a cheerful greeting with visitors or display on your wall to bring a bit of sunshine indoors.

The cutting on this project is not difficult. The leaf sections and flower petals are cut from the same piece of wood, so the pieces fit together perfectly. A little fitting is required for the center of the flowers and the leaf sections. The more accurate your cuts, the easier it will be to assemble the final project.

For this design, I use yellowheart (or satinwood) for the sunflowers, black walnut for the sunflower centers, and cherry for the leaves.

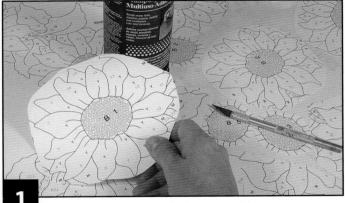

1 **Prepare the patterns.** Make four copies of the pattern. Keep a master copy for future use. Cut the sections of the pattern apart. Tape a piece of clear contact paper to a board. Apply spray adhesive to the pattern pieces and position them on the shiny side of the contact paper. Cut the pattern pieces apart.

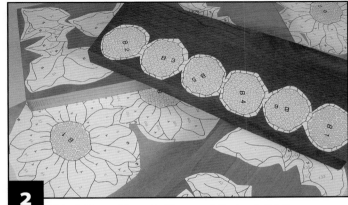

2 **Attach the patterns to the wood.** Peel and stick the pattern pieces onto your wood. Grain direction is not a large factor in this pattern. Position the patterns closely together to make use of as much of the expensive hardwoods as possible. The leaf sections and flower petals can be cut in large sections.

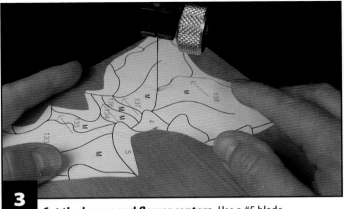

3 **Cut the leaves and flower centers.** Use a #5 blade. Make sure your blade is square to the saw table. Flat wood is important for a good cut and fit. Plane the wood if necessary. Number the back of each piece with a pencil as you cut it free.

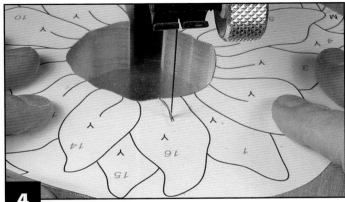

4 **Cut the petal veining lines.** Cut along one petal to the center. Then cut around the center. Cut the veining lines on each petal before cutting the petals free. Cut up to the end of the veining line, then back the blade back out to the flower center.

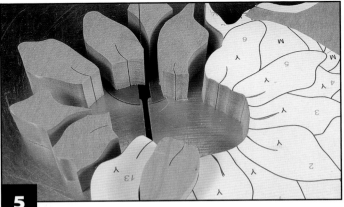

5 **Cut the petals.** Start at one end and work your way around. For easier cutting, skip to the petals where the line continues the whole way around without a sharp stop into another petal, such as petals 2, 5, or 14. You can scroll the petals as small groups, and then cut and number each individual petal.

6 **Dry assemble the wreath.** Position the cut pieces on a full-size pattern attached to a work board. Make any adjustments in fit now. If you do not like the wood color or grain direction of a piece, you can cut a new piece. Mark the areas that you want to sand down, using the shaping guide as a reference.

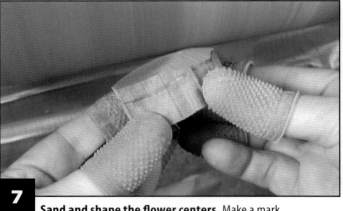

7 **Sand and shape the flower centers.** Make a mark approximately one third of the way down from the top. Sand the edges of the flower center down to the line, and round the top. Work slowly and replace each piece back onto the pattern often. I use pneumatic sanding drums.

8 **Shape the first flower.** Replace the center to the working board. Make a line on the inside of the petals equal with the edge of the flower center. Sand down to this line on the drum sander. Round and shape each petal using the pattern as a guide. Sand carefully; you can't add more wood if you sand too much.

9 **Sand the remaining sections.** Work your way around the wreath from the first flower. Start with the lowest piece of the section first. Taper the ends of the stems for a flowing look. Mark the pieces on adjacent sections to help achieve a consistent flow.

10 **Texture the center of the flowers.** Drill a series of holes (I use an ¹¹⁄₆₄"-diameter bit) in the flower centers. This will make each center look as if it is loaded with sunflower seeds. Experiment on scrap wood until you are happy with the hole placement.

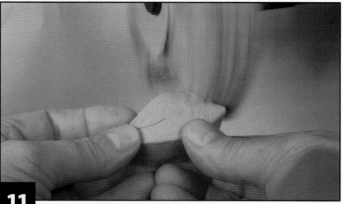

11 **Finish sanding the pieces.** Buff each piece with a 220-grit sanding mop. The sanding mop removes any scratches left from the shaping process and gives an attractive sheen to each piece that will help the gel varnish go on smoothly.

12 **Apply the finish.** Paint a layer of natural gel varnish onto the top and sides of each piece. Let the varnish set for five minutes, then wipe it off with a soft rag. Allow the finish to dry overnight, then apply another coat. Clean out any grooves with a dental tool.

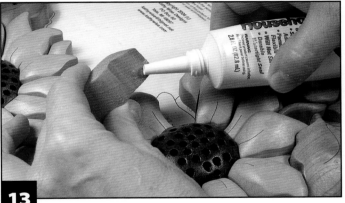

13 **Tack pieces together into small sections.** For easier assembly, dry assemble the wreath, then tack small sections together with cyanoacrylate (CA) glue or 100% silicone caulk.

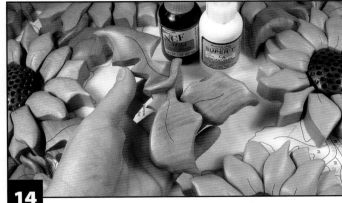

14 **Tack the small sections together.** Create four main sections (such as a sunflower and one side of leaves) to be glued to the backing board. Continue to use CA glue or silicone caulk.

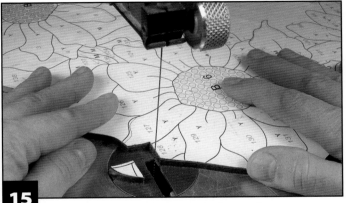

15 **Cut the backing board.** Position the four sections on the work board and trace the perimeter onto the full pattern. Transfer the pattern to a piece of ¼"-thick plywood or masonite. Cut ¹⁄₁₆" inside the line you just drew. Buff the edges with a mop sander, then stain the edges as desired.

16 **Finish the wreath.** Apply wood glue or 5-minute epoxy to the back of the sections and position them on the backing board. Space the sections for fit if needed. Saturate your rag with gel varnish and wring it out well. Lightly rub the wreath with the rag. Attach a mirror-style hanger to the back of the wreath.

Materials & Tools

Materials:
- 1" x 4" x 13" black walnut or dark wood of choice (flower centers)
- 1" x 8" x 34" yellowheart, satinwood, or yellow wood of choice (flower petals)
- 1" x 12" x 13" cherry or medium-toned wood of choice (leaves)
- ¼" x 18" x 18" plywood or Masonite (backing board)
- Spray adhesive
- Yellow wood glue or epoxy
- Cyanoacrylate glue or 100% silicone caulk
- Clear shelf contact paper
- Natural gel varnish
- Wiping rags, disposable brushes, and cotton swabs
- Mirror-style hanger

Tools:
- #5 reverse-tooth blades or blades of choice
- Drill with ¹¹⁄₆₄"-diameter bit or bit size of choice
- Pneumatic-drum sanders (8"-diameter drum with 120-grit sandpaper and 2"-diameter drum with 220-grit sandpaper)
- 220-grit sanding mop
- Dental tool (to clean grooves)

CUTTING NOTES:

The sunflower petals are cut from a single piece of wood, so grain direction is not a factor.

Number all your petals and leaves on the back as you cut them. This will make placing them back onto the pattern for fitting and finishing much easier.

Legend

Start with 1" wood

⟵————— Grain direction

M...........Medium shade of brown wood, greenish if possible

Y.............Yellow shade of wood

B.............Black or dark wood of your choice

◯ ....Drill ¼" deep holes for seeds

Photocopy at 165%

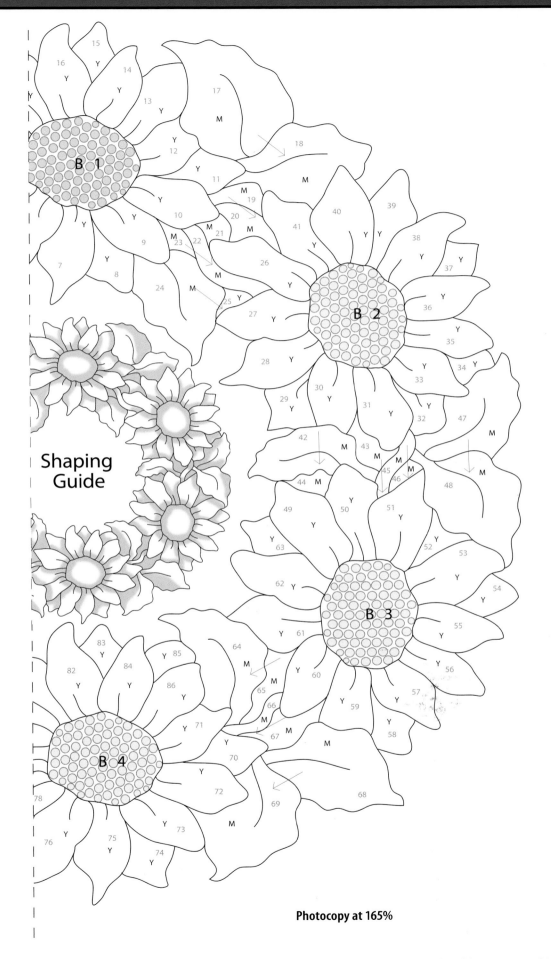

Shaping Guide

Photocopy at 165%

Creating a Lighthouse Scene

By Janette Square

This project is based on a photo I took of the Cape Blanco lighthouse in Port Orford, Ore.

I added rocks and water for interest, but tried to recreate the peaceful feeling of the isolated lighthouse. Modify the design by adding stripes or changing the colors to personalize the project.

Cutting the Pieces

Select and lay out your wood choices. Pay attention to the grain direction and colors. The area between the grass and rocks is an excellent opportunity to use the figure of the wood to portray windswept sand. Choose wild grain patterns in various colors for the rocks.

Drill blade-entry holes in the window openings. Use a #7 blade to cut the larger sections of the structures including the roof. Switch to a #5 blade for the smaller pieces, such as the windows and trim.

Shaping the Lighthouse

Start shaping the intarsia with the house. I use a belt sander for the large flat areas and sand the smaller pieces by hand. Sand the windows and doors to fit slightly lower than the surrounding buildings. Use shims to raise the foundation and the trim pieces on the roof and windows. Leave the white trim around the door slightly higher than the walls.

Round the lighthouse tower with a flexible-drum sander and match the contour of the grey pieces to the contour of the main tower. The right-hand piece of the window is slightly beveled toward the left to create the proper angle.

The most difficult area to shape is around the lighthouse bulb. Use an oscillating spindle sander to shape the concave pieces beside the bulb. You want to create the illusion of a piece of glass going behind the light. Taper the ceiling above the bulb to appear as if the bottom is behind the bulb.

Ease the edges of the pieces by hand sanding with 220-grit sandpaper. Then buff the pieces with a sanding mop. Glue the house and lighthouse tower pieces together.

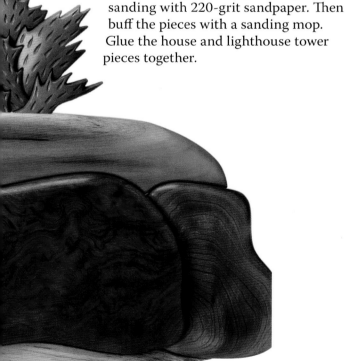

This intarsia design is inspired by a photo of the Cape Blanco lighthouse in Port Orford, Ore.

Shaping the Landscape

Shape the grass area next, followed by the sand. Use a spindle sander to contour the sand so it appears to be indented under the overhanging grass. Use the spindle sander to create curves and gouges in the rocks. Use shims to raise the rocks in the foreground.

Shape the water and bush with a drum sander. Add texture to the bush with a rotary power carver and carving bit. Glue the landscape pieces together.

Finishing the Intarsia

Dry fit the pieces together to ensure a good fit, then glue large sections together for easier finishing. Apply clear gel varnish or your finish of choice. Remove the excess finish with paper towels. Use an air compressor and rubber dental pick for tight areas. Let the finish dry overnight and apply a second coat.

Glue the sections together and trace around the project onto a piece of ⅛"-thick plywood. Cut the plywood backing board approximately ⅛" inside the traced line with a #3 blade. Glue the intarsia to the backing board with wood glue. Attach a hanger, list the woods used, and sign your work.

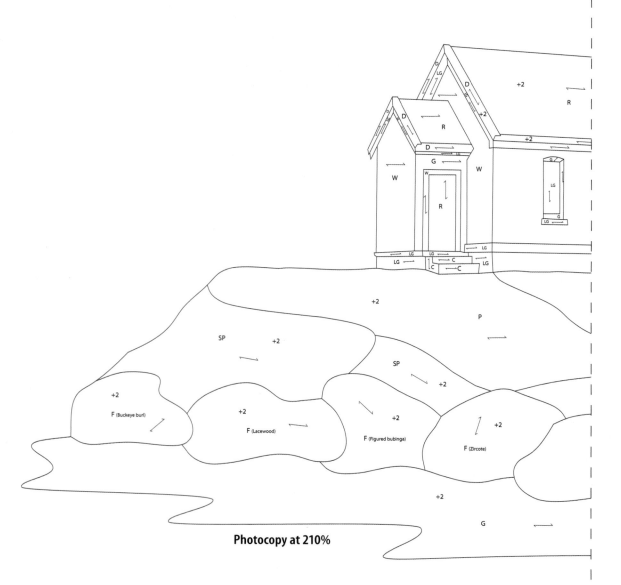

Photocopy at 210%

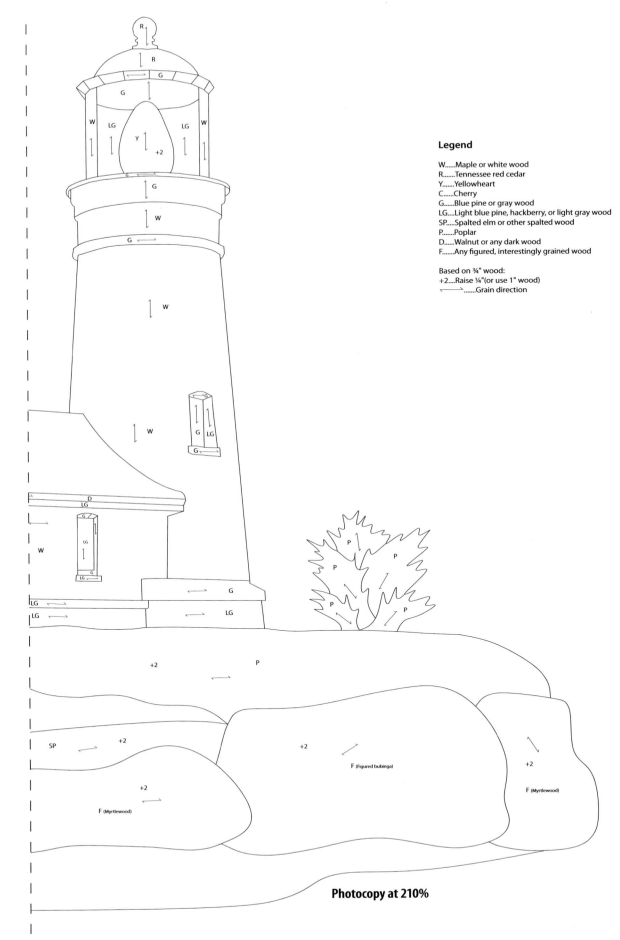

Legend

W......Maple or white wood
R.......Tennessee red cedar
Y.......Yellowheart
C......Cherry
G......Blue pine or gray wood
LG....Light blue pine, hackberry, or light gray wood
SP.....Spalted elm or other spalted wood
P.......Poplar
D......Walnut or any dark wood
F.......Any figured, interestingly grained wood

Based on ¾" wood:
+2....Raise ¼"(or use 1" wood)
⟵⟶ ....Grain direction

Photocopy at 210%

Place the cut pieces on a full-size copy of the pattern.

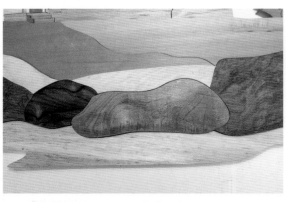

Choose wood with interesting colors and figures for the rocks.

Create the illusion of glass going behind the light by shaping concave pieces.

Use a rotary power carver to add texture to the bush.

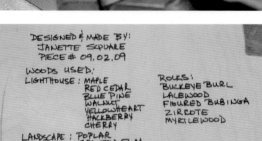

Sign the back of your project and list the types of wood used for each area.

Materials & Tools

Materials:

(The woods listed are based on my finished project. I encourage you to use what you have available and personalize the project.)

- ¾" x 9" x 12" hard maple (white areas)
- 1" x 3" x 10" Tennessee red cedar (roof)
- ¾" x 3" x 12" hackberry (around light and windows)
- ¾" x 10" x 12" several shades of blue pine (building accents and window trim)
- ¾" x 4" x 22" blue pine (water)
- ¾" x 2" x 2" cherry (steps)
- 1" x 2" x 2" yellowheart (lightbulb)
- 1" x 2" x 7" walnut (building trim)
- ¾" x 4" x 4" green poplar (shrub)
- ¾" x 4" x 22" green poplar (grass)
- 1" x 7" x 8" spalted elm (sand)
- Woods used for rocks are as follows from left to right: buckeye burl, lacewood, figured bubinga, zircote, and myrtlewood
- ⅛" to ¼"-thick scrap wood (risers)
- ⅛" to ¼" x 20" x 24" plywood (backing board)
- Fine-point permanent marker
- Clear packing tape
- Spray adhesive
- Sandpaper, 220 grit
- Assorted grit sanding drums
- Wood glue
- Clear satin gel varnish or finish of choice
- Hanger
- Disposable foam brush

Tools:

- #3, #5, and #7 reverse-tooth blades or blades of choice
- Flexible-drum sander
- Oscillating spindle sander
- Belt sander
- Sanding mop
- Drill press for sanding mop (optional)
- Rotary power carver with assorted carving bits
- Air compressor and/or rubber tipped dental tools (to remove excess finish)
- Drill with ⅛"-diameter drill bit

Fall Leaf Frame

By Kathy Wise

Welcome fall with this set of 5" by 7" picture frames. This pattern is designed to be stack cut with three different colors of wood, mixed and matched to create three frames. I used ⅜"-thick black walnut, maple, and mahogany. Use the colors and types of wood of your choice.

The pattern can be sanded two different ways, as shown here. One way is to sand in levels as you would any intarsia piece for a 3-D feel. The other way is to simply finish sand with a sanding mop to slightly round the edges. You decide if you want a fretwork back board for a desk frame or the plain back board for a wall-hung frame.

The pieces are stack cut, so they will fit together perfectly when you mix up your leaves for each of the three frames. Canadian scrollers may try red and white woods for a patriotic maple leaf frame.

This is a very forgiving pattern. If you stray off the line slightly it doesn't matter, as you have the same cut on all the pieces.

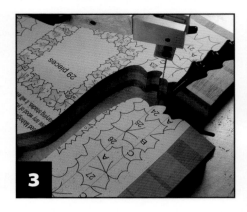

TIP **RUBBER FINGER TIPS**

I sand most of my small pieces on a pneumatic drum sander, and my fingers usually pay the price. I found that if I wear the rubber finger tips found at office supply stores (they come in at least 3 sizes), I save a lot of skin. They also help you hold the small parts so they don't slip out of your hands.

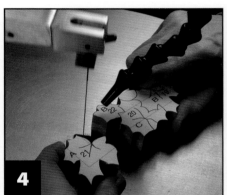

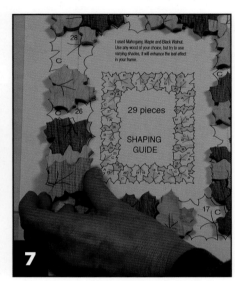

Step 1: Make six copies of the pattern. Always keep a master copy to use later. Tape contact paper flat on a board. Spray adhesive on the pattern, and attach the pattern to the contact paper. Cut out the pattern piece attached to the contact paper. Plane the wood pieces of your choice to ⅜" thickness. Peel the backing off the contact paper, and attach it to the wood.

Step 2: Use double-sided carpet tape to attach the three layers of wood together. I clamped the boards together so they were nice and flat and taped the edges with clear tape. If three layers are too thick for you to cut easily, try using only two layers.

Step 3: Cut out all of the pieces using a scroll saw with a #5 blade or your blade of choice. Make sure your blade is square to the saw table by using a small square or angle to check the first piece you cut. Start by cutting the frame into four smaller sections for easier handling.

Step 4: Cut the outside edges away from the leaf section, skipping the deep indentations. Go back and cut the indentations with two cuts, one from each direction. Cut off each leaf, working from one end of each section, marking each stacked piece with the number on the pattern piece. It is important to work slowly when stack cutting so you do not bend the blade—which will give you sloped cuts on your leaves, making it hard to assemble.

Step 5: Cut out backer boards. Use ordinary double-sided tape to stick three ¼"-thick boards together for stack cutting, again taping the edges with clear packaging tape. If your frames are going on a wall, just cut out the plain back board. If you are making desktop frames, use the fretwork pattern and frame support for a different look. Drill blade-entry holes for the fretwork designs, and cut them out. Then stack and cut the three spacers and the three front frames that the leaves will be glued

to (see pattern). Finally, if you are making the desk frame, cut out two frame supports for each frame.

Step 6: Glue the leaf supports and spacers to the back boards. Clamp, and allow them to dry overnight. Sand the edges on a belt sander and buff them with a sanding mop. Pull apart all pieces of the stacked leaves. You may need to insert a flat, skinny tool of some sort (such as a small chisel or utility knife blade) between the layers to separate them.

Step 7: Lay out the pieces and mix up woods according to the A, B, and C markings on the patterns. For the first frame: A = maple, B = black walnut, and C = mahogany. The second frame: A= black walnut, B = mahogany, and C = maple. The third frame: A = mahogany, B = maple, and C = black walnut—or arrange them to your liking. Once you have all the frames laid out in the correct order, mark them according to what frame they belong to. This will ensure you don't mix up your leaves when sanding and finishing. If you are making desk frames, mark in the middle with a pencil, so the markings will not show on the back edges.

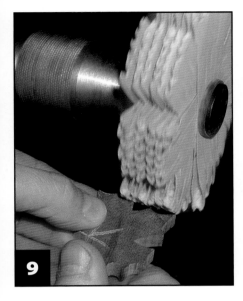

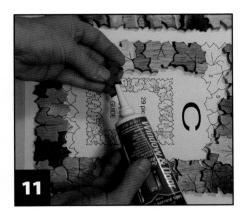

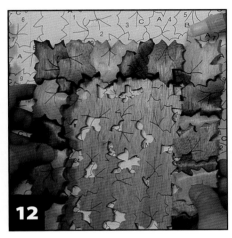

Materials & Tools

Materials:

I used these woods on my frames, but you can use your materials of choice.
- ⅜" x 10" x 9" black walnut (leaves)
- ⅜" x 10" x 9" maple (leaves)
- ⅜" x 10" x 9" mahogany (leaves)
- ¼" x 8" x 5' plywood or planed wood of your choice (backer board, spacers, leaf supports, and frame supports)
- Roll of clear shelf contact paper
- Spray adhesive
- Yellow wood glue
- Double-sided carpet tape
- Double-sided tape
- 100% silicone glue
- Clear gel varnish
- Wiping rags
- 3 each sawtooth hangers (optional)
- 2 small screws (optional)

Tools:
- #5 or #3 reverse-tooth blades or blades of choice
- Pneumatic drum-sander
- Sanding map
- Small, round paint brush

Step 8: Use a pneumatic-drum sander to shape and sand each leaf. Use the shaping guide as a reference, and mark the excess wood you want to remove with a pencil. Be careful not to take too much off the side of the leaves that run along the outside frame. Replace pieces back into the project often to check how much wood you are removing and re-mark as needed. You want to achieve depth and shadows in your leaves. If you choose not to shape and want to simply round the edges, go right to the next step.

Step 9: Buff the pieces with a sanding mop to slightly round all the edges and give the wood a nice, polished look. Buff the back boards and frame supports as well.

Step 10: Use a soft, round paintbrush to apply clear gel varnish to all your pieces. Carefully cover the top, bottom, and all the side edges. Let it dry for five minutes, wipe it off with a clean rag, let it dry throughly, then apply a second coat and let it dry overnight. For a faster finish, dip the fretwork back in regular varnish and blow out the excess varnish with an air gun, instead of trying to brush it on.

Step 11: Lay out your pieces on the patterns taped to a flat board. Tack the entire frame together with clear 100% silicone glue and let dry overnight. This makes gluing easier and faster—and the pieces don't slide out of position. Place all the pieces on the pattern while tacking them together for an exact fit. Apply two or three very small drops of silicone to the edges, press them together, and allow it to dry overnight. Don't let it squeeze up

through the cracks—wipe it off with a toothpick if it does. The silicone will give a little when you glue it to the backer board.

Step 12: Glue the leaves to the backer boards with yellow wood glue. Stack sandbags on top of the pieces. Let them dry overnight. If you are making desk frames, glue the frame supports on each side of the back. Be sure to have the support extend slightly beyond the backer board so the frame sits correctly. Drill and add a small screw if you choose. Allow it to dry overnight.

Step 13: Put a final wipe of gel varnish on the entire piece at this point. Saturate your wiping rag, and wring it out. Use just a light rub. Don't get a lot on the piece, or you will have to spend time cleaning the excess out of the cracks. Attach a sawtooth hanger if you are hanging your frames.

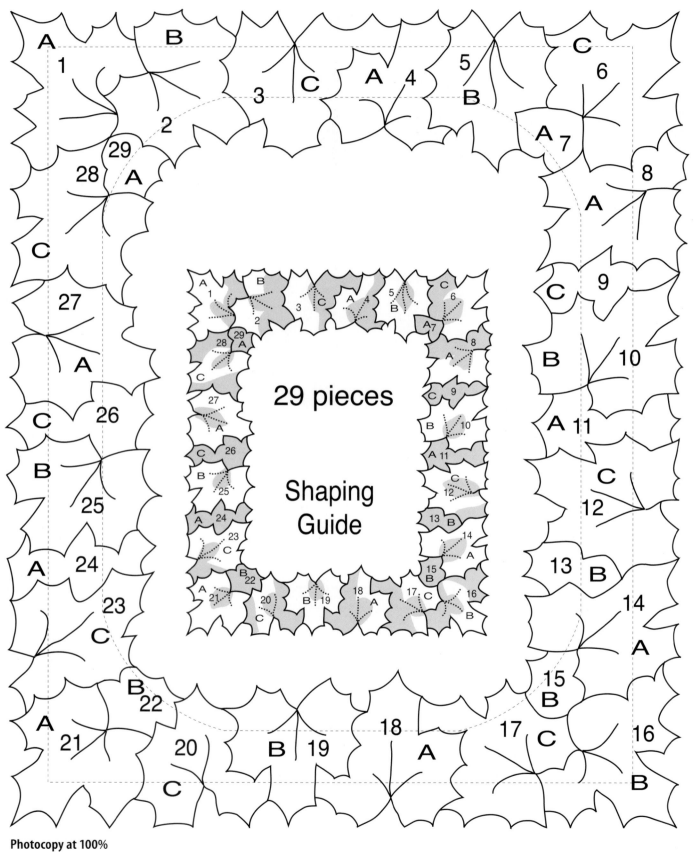

29 pieces

Shaping
Guide

Photocopy at 100%

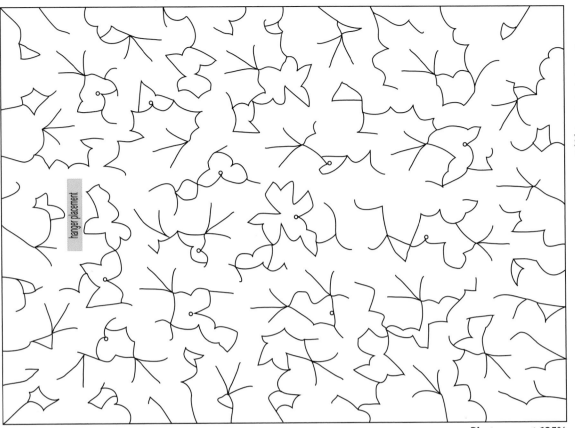

hanger placement

Back Board (ignore fretwork markings if you prefer a plain backer)

Photocopy at 135%

Stack 3 shades of wood (⅜");
cut out and mix up leaves for
a fall color look. Makes 3 frames.

Cut 3 each of the following:
back board, spacer, leaf support,
and frame support. Stacking 3
layers of wood will allow you to
cut most efficiently.

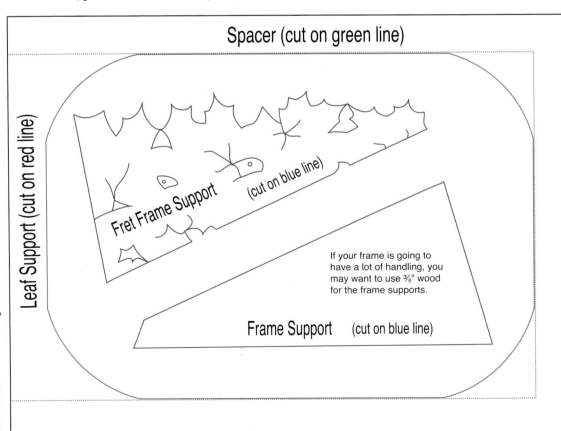

Spacer (cut on green line)

Leaf Support (cut on red line)

Fret Frame Support (cut on blue line)

If your frame is going to
have a lot of handling, you
may want to use ⅜" wood
for the frame supports.

Frame Support (cut on blue line)

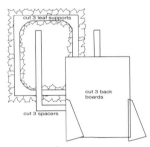

cut 3 leaf supports

cut 3 back boards

cut 3 spacers

If you prefer, you can
use ⅛" thick plywood
for the back pieces for
a thinner frame.

Leaf supports _____

Frame supports _____

Spacers ....

Photocopy at 135%

Create this beautiful intarsia frame without the use of miters or joints.

Without the intarsia roses, it is a simple contemporary frame.

Frame Your Photos with Intarsia Roses

Embellish this quick and easy frame with stunning hardwood flowers

By Kathy Wise

Special occasions demand special gifts. This rose frame makes an elegant wedding gift and is perfect for displaying portraits without overpowering them.

The base frame is made of gently curved sections and eliminates the need for mitered cuts or difficult joints. Beginners can eliminate the intarsia roses and use figured wood to create a stylish contemporary frame. The rose embellishment requires minimal cutting and shaping and adds a romantic touch, giving the frame a more traditional feel. The spacer is open on top, so you can easily slide a photo in place.

Make four photocopies of the pattern. Keep a master copy for later use. Cut the individual pattern pieces, apply spray adhesive to the back, and adhere them to the shiny side of the contact paper. Contact paper sticks well to the wood, but it is easy to remove and replace if you want to change the position of the pattern. It pulls off easily when you are done cutting and doesn't leave a residue on the wood. Cut each pattern piece free from the sheet of contact paper.

Plane any wood that is not flat. Peel and stick the pattern pieces onto your wood of choice. Line the arrows up with the direction of the grain.

TIP | **SQUARE CUTS**

If your blade is not square to the saw table, the intarsia pieces will not fit tightly together. Check a cut piece with a square to make sure the blade is square to the table.

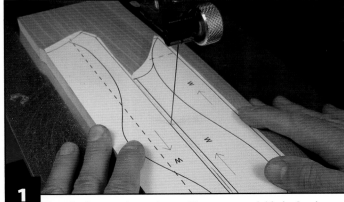

1 **Cut the frame pieces.** I use a #3 reverse-tooth blade. Sand the straight edges with a belt sander or flat drum sander so the edges are smooth and flat.

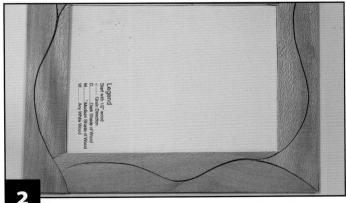

2 **Check the fit of the frame pieces.** Position the cut frame pieces on a copy of the pattern and check the fit. Make any required adjustments.

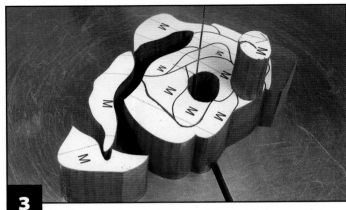

3 **Cut the intarsia embellishment.** Start with the roses. Cut in from the side to cut the middle sections first. This gives you more wood to hold as you cut the small sections. Cut the leaves and number the back of all of the pieces as you cut them.

4 **Prepare the pieces for shaping.** Place the cut pieces on a full-size pattern taped to a board. Check the fit of each piece and adjust as needed. Use a pencil and the shaping guide to shade the areas to sand on each piece.

5 **Sand and shape the pieces.** Shape the pieces with an 80-grit sanding drum and smooth the pieces with a 220-grit sanding drum. Replace the pieces back on the pattern often to check the fit and flow. Round the edges of the frame pieces.

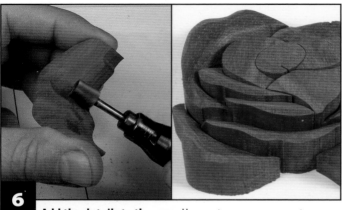

6 **Add the details to the rose.** Use a rotary power carver to add details to the petals. Put a sharp angle on the inside edge of the petals. Place the petal next to the other pieces to see how it looks in relation to the others.

7 **Buff the pieces.** I use a 220-grit sanding mop to remove any remaining scratches and give the pieces a nice sheen without changing the shape. Buff all of the pieces with the mop. The varnish finish is easier to apply on the buffed wood.

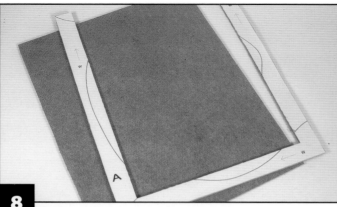

8 **Cut the spacer and backing board.** Stack cut the perimeter of the two pieces for the backing board and spacer. Separate the stack and cut along the dotted lines on the top blank to make the spacer. Glue the spacer to the backing board with wood glue.

9 **Assemble the frame.** Apply cyanoacrylate (CA) glue to one piece and accelerator to the adjoining piece. Quickly press the pieces together. Start with the side pieces and then join the assembled sides at the corners. If there is a gap in the frame, position it in the right bottom corner, which will be covered by the rose. Sand the back of the frame to make sure it is flat.

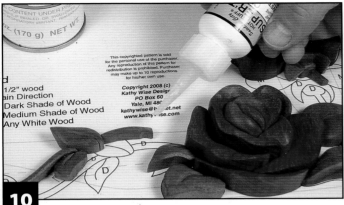

10 **Assemble the intarsia.** Glue the pieces together into four sections. Apply accelerator to one piece and CA glue to the adjoining piece. Join the pieces over a flat surface to ensure the bottom is flush. Wiggle the pieces as the glue sets to keep them from sticking to the surface. Sand the bottom of the pieces flat.

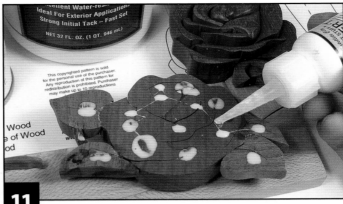

11 **Glue the intarsia embellishment to the frame.** Add dots of wood glue to the corner rose and add a few dots of CA glue between the wood glue. Spray accelerator on the frame and press the rose firmly in place. Use the same technique to attach the other sections to the frame.

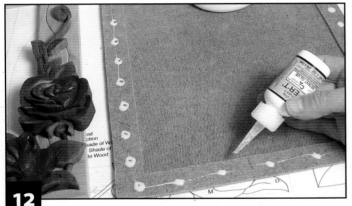

12 **Attach the frame to the backing board.** Add wood glue to the spacer and add drops of CA glue between the wood glue. Spray accelerator on the back of the frame. Press the frame firmly in place. Sand or bevel the edges of the backing board with a router to make sure it is not visible from the front.

13 **Apply a finish.** I use a spray satin varnish. Apply a coat, allow it to dry, and then apply a second coat. Attach your hanger of choice to the back. You can use a mirror-style hanger or attach two screw eyes and string a hanging wire between the screw eyes. Be sure to sign and date your work.

Materials & Tools

Materials:

These are the woods I use, but you can use your woods of choice.

- ½" x 5" x 10" dark wood such as black walnut (leaves)
- ½" x 10" x 15" white or light wood such as sycamore (frame)
- ½" x 4" x 6" red wood such as bloodwood (roses)
- ¼" x 30" x 12" plywood or fiberboard (backing board and spacer)
- Roll of clear shelf contact paper
- Spray adhesive
- Yellow wood glue
- Spray varnish

- Cyanoacrylate glue and accelerator
- Mirror-style hanger or screw eyes and wire

Tools:

- #3 reverse-tooth blades or blades of choice
- Pneumatic-drum sander with 80- and 220-grit sleeves
- Die grinder or rotary power carver with cutter
- 220-grit sanding mop

Shaping
Guide

Overlay roses
and leaves

Photocopy at 140%

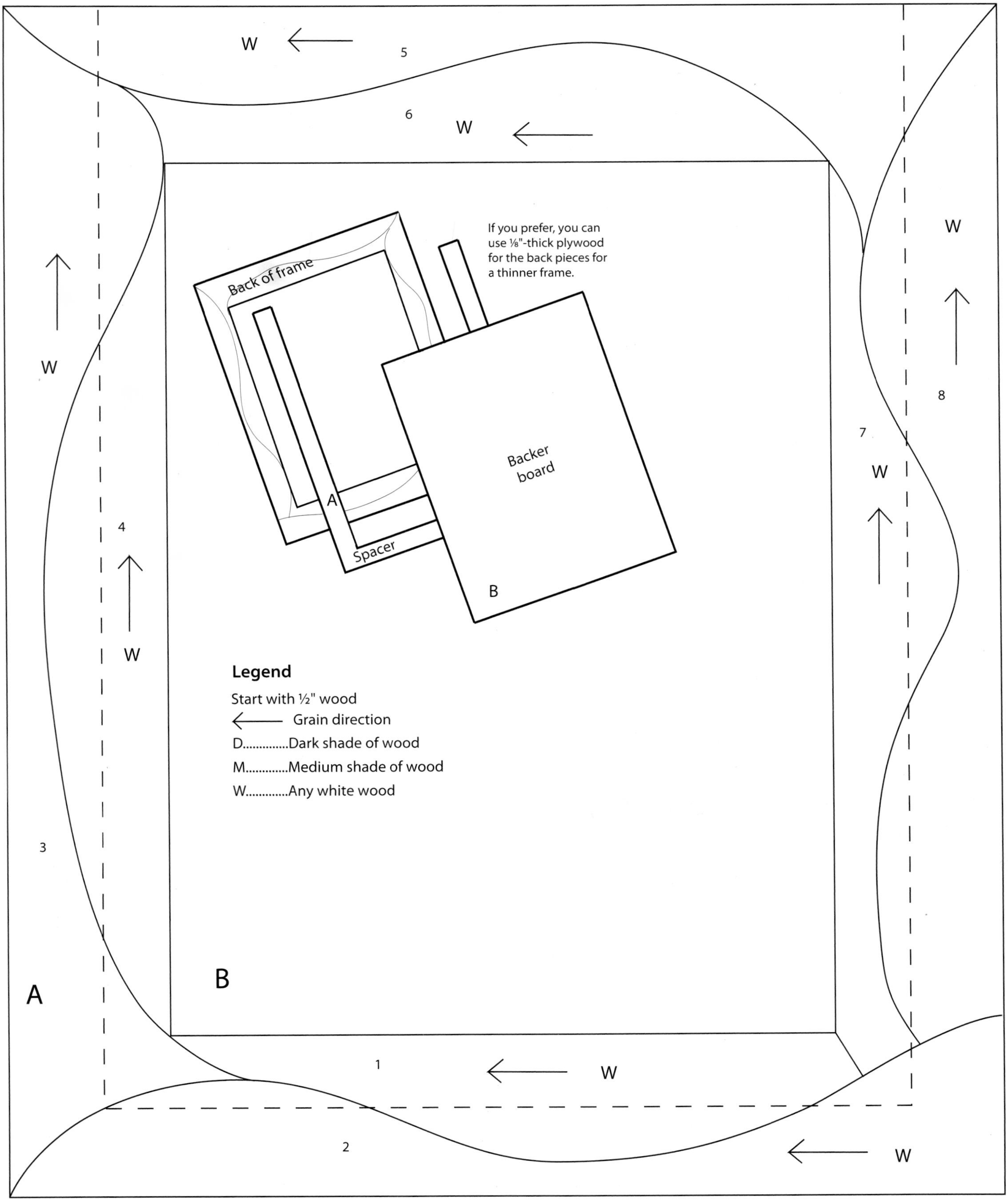

W ← 5

6 W ←

If you prefer, you can use ⅛"-thick plywood for the back pieces for a thinner frame.

Back of frame

W

W ↑

W ↑

A

Spacer

Backer board

B

W ↓

W ↑

8

7

4

W ↑

W ↑

Legend

Start with ½" wood

←———— Grain direction

D.............Dark shade of wood

M.............Medium shade of wood

W.............Any white wood

3

A

B

1 ← W

2

← W

Photocopy at 140%

Intarsia Autumn Gobbler

By Kathy Wise

Hunters are always looking for new and unique way to display their trophies. This intarsia gobbler allows you to show off your skills in the field and in the shop—all in one handsome display.

If you don't have a turkey hunter in the family, the piece can be cut completely in wood for an outstanding Thanksgiving decoration. In addition to the versatility of cutting the project with or without the tail and beard, you can also cut the design in fewer pieces for an easier pattern.

Start by deciding which turkey design you want to make. It can be made with as few as 27 pieces (without the wooden tail feathers) or as many as 216. Make sure all your stock is flat—plane or sand it if necessary.

You could easily adapt this pattern into a unique turkey mount, as shown here.

TIP **USE A LIGHT WASH OF COLOR TO TINT WOOD**

It is sometimes necessary to stain or tint the wood to achieve the right look for a finished piece. This turkey would not look like a strutting turkey unless the head was a brighter red and blue. I applied a light red wash over the burled cherry, using watered-down acrylic paint. I did the same with the bird's-eye maple with a very light blue wash. Practice on a scrap piece of wood to get the right color. Let the wash dry completely overnight and finish with clear gel varnish. You can also use oil paint mixed with the varnish. Remember not to make the paint too thick; you want the wood grain to show though. This is a tint, not solid paint. Wood dye can be used as well.

TIP SANDING LARGER

Tape the large body sections toge[ther]
duct tape on both sides; this holds [it]
together enough so you can round the
edges of each section. You can also attach
the pieces to a thin wooden sanding
shim, using double-sided tape. I use the
duct tape method because it is quick,
but depending on the piece I am
shaping, I may use a sanding
shim. On the tail sections
I used a dot or two of
cyanoacrylate (CA) glue and
mild accelerator to hold the
pieces together for sanding.
Just use a few drops of CA
glue on the bottom seam
and spray with accelerator.
This will let you sand the
feathers evenly. To break
the pieces apart, rap
them sharply on a
hard surface.

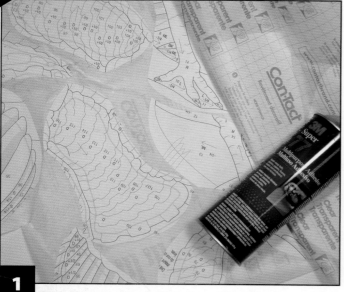

1 **Prepare your patterns.** Make six to eight copies of the pattern. Always keep a master copy. Cut out the pattern pieces, and group them into colors. Tape the contact paper flat on a board. Spray adhesive on the pattern pieces, and stick them to the contact paper. After all your pieces are adhered to the contact paper, cut out each paper pattern piece.

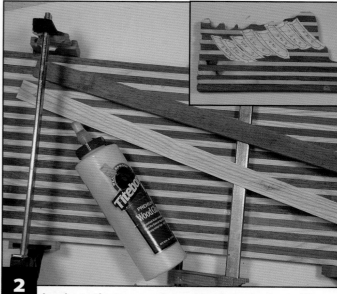

2 **Laminate the two woods to make the striped wood for feathers (optional).** On a table saw, cut 1"-thick black walnut into ⅜"-wide strips and 1"-thick poplar or ash in ¼"-wide strips. Alternate colors, using wood glue, clamp together, and let dry overnight. Plane or sand the laminated wood slightly until it is flat. Using a turkey photo for reference, peel and stick pattern pieces on your striped wood, laying each feather on a slant. Stagger the patterns, or you will lose the individual feather look. You could achieve a similar effect by woodburning dark stripes onto feathers cut out of white poplar or ash.

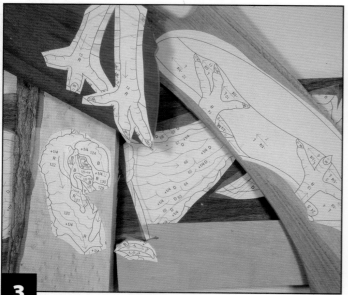

3 **Peel and stick the pattern pieces onto the stock.** Use the arrows to determine the grain direction. The nine large body pieces are laid out in groups, and the smaller pieces are cut from each section; this way your pattern will fit perfectly, and it is much easier to cut. The large body pieces can be left whole or can be cut along the dotted lines for a more detailed turkey piece.

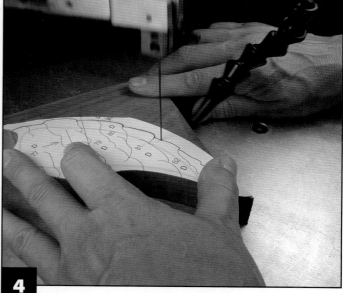

4 **Cut out the pieces.** Make sure your blade is square to the saw table by using a small square to check a cut piece. After you cut each piece, number its back with a pencil. I use a #7 blade when cutting the thicker wood, on the larger main body sections, and on any straight or gently-curved pieces. This helps keep the sides straight without a lot of effort or problems with blade bending. Then I cut out all the smaller pieces within each section with a #5 blade for more curved and sharp turns. If you stray off the line slightly on these detail cuts, they will still fit perfectly together.

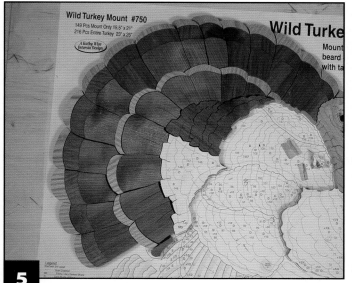

5 **Assemble the cut pieces on a full-sized pattern taped to ¼"-thick plywood.** This layout board will be used later for the backer board. Check for fit and make adjustments as needed. If you do not like the wood color or grain direction you see, change it now.

6 **Rough-sand the large body sections.** Sanding is critical to make your intarsia seem three-dimensional. I use a 4"-diameter pneumatic-drum sander to take off most of the extra wood. Use a pencil to mark the depths you want on the sides of each piece. Sand the wood down to your line. Work slowly and replace each piece onto the pattern and next to the other pieces often. This will make it easier to adjust each piece. Finish sanding with a 2"-diameter pneumatic drum and fine-grit sandpaper. The 2"-diameter drum is also useful to shape the smaller, curved pieces.

7 **Shape the smaller areas.** In the inside cuts and other areas where you can't use a drum sander, use a small grinder and a wood-shaping burr or a rotary power carver and a ½"-diameter sanding drum. I used a carving knife to notch the body feathers and legs. Buff each piece with a 220-grit (or finer) sanding mop. The mop will polish each piece and makes the finish coat of gel varnish go on smoothly. It will also round off any remaining sharp edges.

8 **Apply a natural gel varnish finish to all the pieces.** Use a soft white rag to hand wipe the varnish on the top and side edges. Use a small brush to apply the varnish to any detailed section or deeply-grooved pieces. Allow the varnish to set for about five minutes, and wipe it off. Allow it to dry overnight before applying another coat of varnish. Allow the second coat to dry, and use a piece of wire or a dental tool to gently clean the finish out of the cut in the middle of each feather.

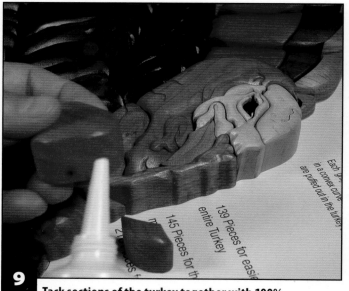

9 **Tack sections of the turkey together with 100% silicone glue.** This makes it much easier to glue your turkey together. If you need to take it apart to adjust a piece, it will break apart easily. Place the pieces on the pattern, and tack the feathers and body sections together in sections, taking care to follow the pattern closely. I have about 25 tacked sections when I am done. Just use one or two drops of silicone per piece, being careful not to let it push up the seam between the tacked pieces. Let it dry overnight.

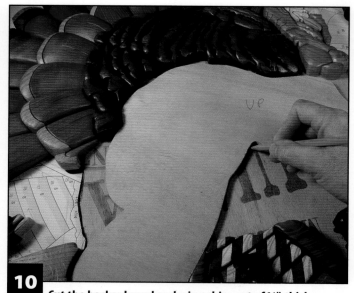

10 **Cut the backer board and wing shim out of ¼"-thick plywood.** Cut ¹⁄₁₆" inside the lines of your layout board around the entire perimeter. Sand the edges of the backer board with the sanding mop, and stain just the edge. NOTE: If you are making the Turkey Mount design, have your tail feathers professionally mounted by a taxidermist in the spread-out fan-style, using a resin compound. Cut a backer board to support your tail feather fan. Cut out a second backer board to fit the turkey without the tail feathers and beard. Epoxy the resin part of the fan to the tail board. Drill a hole in the chest on an upward slant to epoxy the beard into place. Make sure it is hanging at a natural angle. Screw the tail section to the body when all staining is complete.

Materials:

- ¾" x 6" x 18" oak (feather tips)
- ¾" x 8" x 24" cedar (feather bodies)
- 1" x 4" x 8" cherry or burled cherry (head)
- 1" x 6" x 6" maple or bird's eye maple (head)
- ½" x 8" x 24" white oak (base)
- ¾" x 8" x 84" (7') black walnut or any dark wood (body/feathers)
- ¾" x 6" x 6" yellowheart (beak)
- ¾" x 8" x 6" mahogany or reddish wood (legs)
- ¾" x 3" x 3" ebony (eyes, toenails)
- 1" - 1½" x 12" x 14" each ash/ poplar and black walnut to make striped wood for wing feathers (optional)
- ¼" x 20" x 20" plywood (backer board)
- ¼" x 24" x 18" plywood (tail fan backer board—mount only)

Materials & Tools

- Roll of clear shelf contact paper
- Spray adhesive
- Yellow wood glue
- Gel natural varnish
- Wiping rags
- Sawtoothed or ring hanger
- Red and blue paint (oil or acrylic)
- 100% silicone glue

Tools:

- #5 and #7 reverse-tooth blades or blades of choice
- Pneumatic-drum sander
- Rotary power carver with ½"-diameter sanding drum
- Planer (optional)
- Table saw (optional)
- Woodburner (optional)
- Sanding mop
- Small brushes

11 **Glue the silicon glue-tacked sections to your backer board, using yellow wood glue.** Put a coat of glue over the entire backer board. Work quickly to put each tacked section in place. "Float" the pieces to the correct positions, and allow the glue to set for a few minutes. Then break apart the feather sections if needed, and spread them apart slightly to fill any gaps. Insert a thin piece of wood between the pieces, and gently pry them apart. Weigh the pieces down with sandbags, working from the outside edges to the inside. Let the glue dry overnight. Trim any overhanging backer board with a rotary power carver and ½"-diameter sanding drum, and touch up the stained edges. Put a final wipe of gel varnish on the entire piece. Saturate your rag, wring it out, and give the turkey a light rub. Don't get a lot on the piece, or you will have to spend time cleaning out the cracks. Finally, attach a sawtooth hanger or ring hanger.

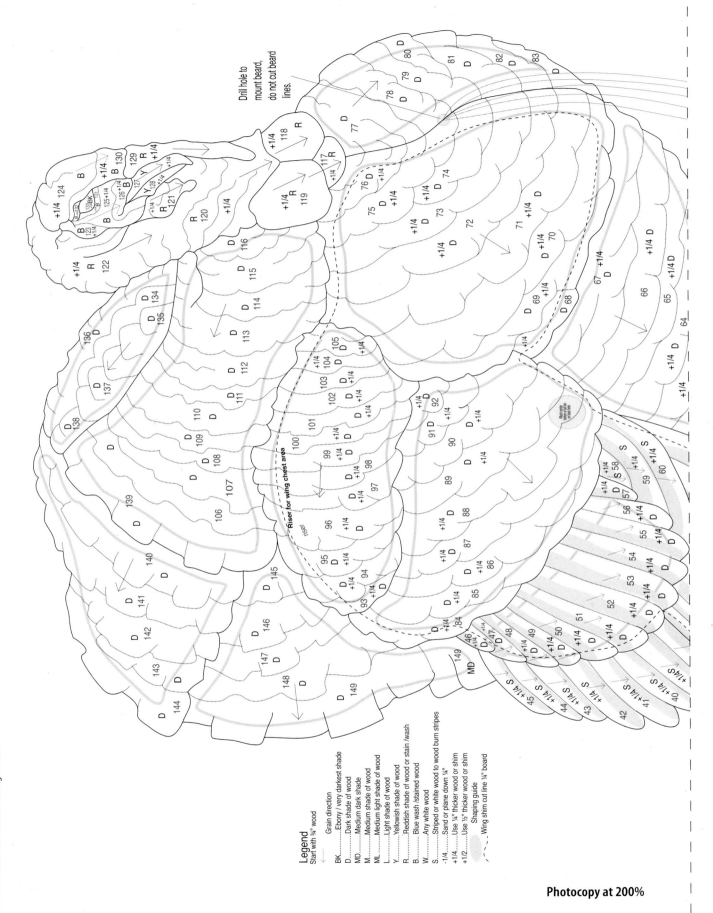

Drill hole to
mount beard,
do not cut beard
lines.

Legend
Start with ¾" wood

→ ....Grain direction
BK............Ebony / very darkest shade
D ....Dark shade of wood
MD............Medium dark shade
M ....Medium shade of wood
ML............Medium light shade of wood
L ....Light shade of wood
Y ....Yellowish shade of wood
R ....Reddish shade of wood or stain /wash
B ....Blue wash /stained wood
W ....Any white wood
S ....Striped or white wood to wood burn stripes
-1/4............Sand or plane down ¼"
+1/4...........Use ¼" thicker wood or shim
+1/2...........Use ½" thicker wood or shim
............Shaping guide
- - - - Wing shim cut line ¾" board

Photocopy at 200%

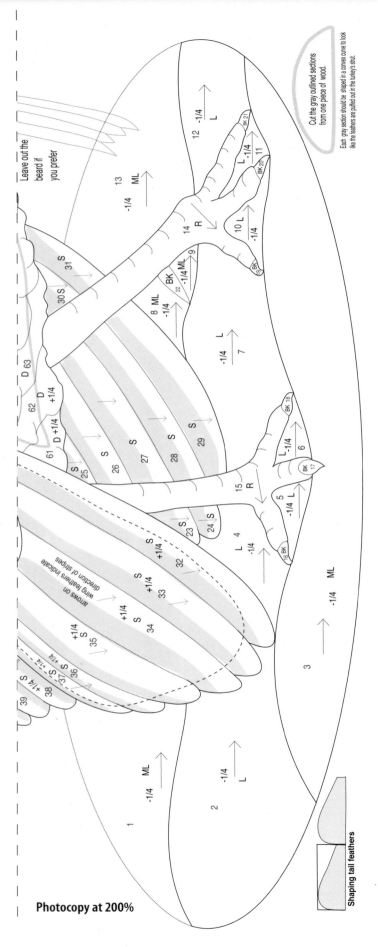

Photocopy at 200%

Leave out the beard if you prefer

Cut the gray outlined sections from one piece of wood.

Each gray section should be shaped in a convex curve to look like the feathers are puffed out in the turkey's strut.

arrows on wing feathers indicate direction of stripes

Shaping tail feathers

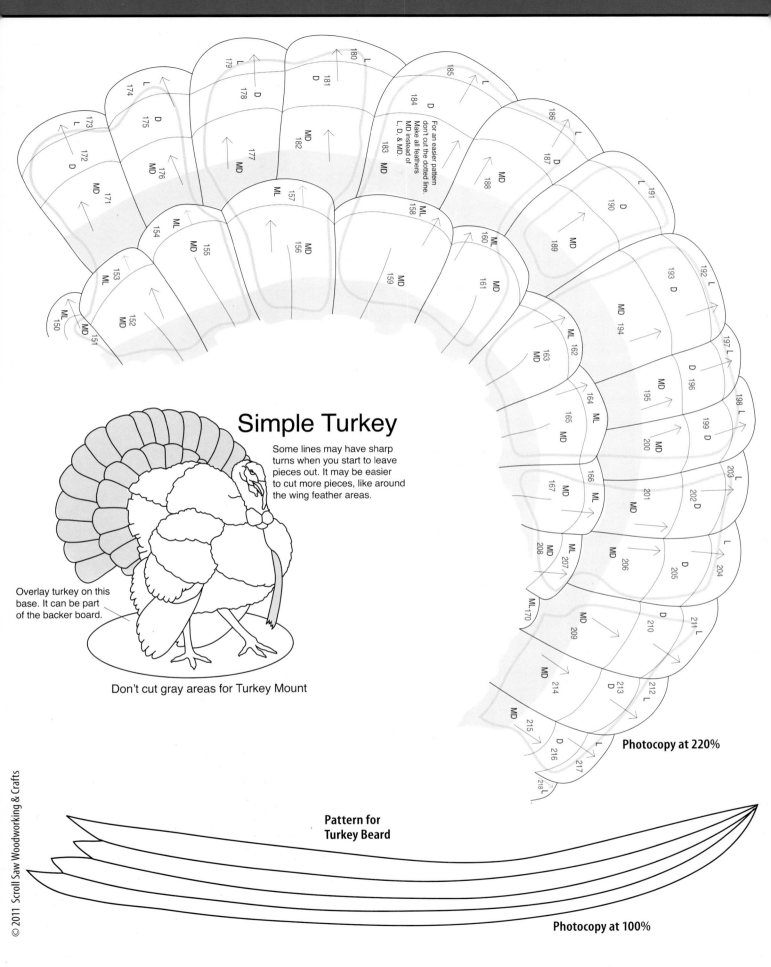

Simple Turkey

Some lines may have sharp turns when you start to leave pieces out. It may be easier to cut more pieces, like around the wing feather areas.

Overlay turkey on this base. It can be part of the backer board.

Don't cut gray areas for Turkey Mount

For an easier pattern don't cut the dotted line. Make all feathers MD instead of L, D, & MD.

Photocopy at 220%

Pattern for Turkey Beard

Photocopy at 100%

Create an Intarsia Scarecrow

By Judy Gale Roberts

I made this cute little character as an homage to the scattered figures decorating gardens and cornfields across the country.

I used walnut for the crows and smile, aspen for the shirt, spalted hackberry for the straw accents, and northern white cedar for the face and hands. All of the other parts are cut from various shades of western red cedar. Make sure your wood is as flat and smooth as possible. Use a thickness planer if necessary.

Number all of the parts on your master pattern and make several photocopies of the pattern. Make all of your copies at the same time. The optics of a copier can change from use to use, and a copy you make at 100% today could reproduce at 99.5% tomorrow.

Cut each pattern piece ⅛" to ¼" outside the lines. This margin gives you time to start cutting on the line correctly before you start cutting the actual part. When the color and grain direction are the same for several adjoining pieces, such as the shirt and pants, leave these patterns connected.

Position the photocopies on the wood to determine the color and grain direction of each piece. Mark the location with small hash marks running from the paper to the wood. Use the hash marks to reposition the pattern back on the wood after you apply the adhesive to the pattern.

Rough shape the entire project before spending a lot of time trying to make it perfect. Once the overall shape is established, you can fine tune the shape of individual pieces. As a general rule, remove wood from the top of the pieces to keep things square and continually mark the depth of adjacent pieces.

The pattern for this matching girl scarecrow is available for purchase at *www.intarsia.com*.

SCARECROW: CUTTING THE PIECES

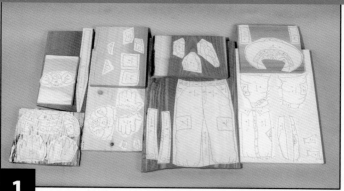

1 **Attach the patterns to the blanks.** Use your method of choice. I use a sticker-making machine that applies adhesive to the back of the pattern. The sticker machine costs more, but the patterns stay securely in place during the cutting process.

2 **Cut the pieces.** Make sure your blade is square to the table. Cut the ¾"-thick wood with a #5 blade. I use a #7 blade for thicker wood and a #0 blade to separate areas, like the shirt, that are cut from a single piece of wood. Keep your blade in the center of the line for the best fit.

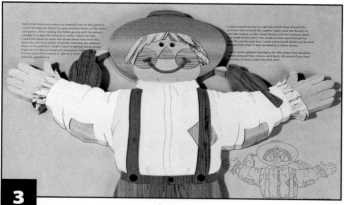

3 **Assemble the pieces.** Sand off any burrs on the bottom and position the pieces on a copy of the pattern. Trim the pieces to adjust the fit or recut pieces as necessary. Number the back of the pieces and remove the pattern. Study the project and formulate a rough plan for shaping and sanding.

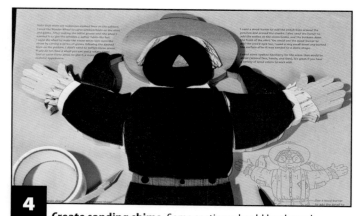

4 **Create sanding shims.** Some sections should be shaped as a unit rather than individually. I create sanding shims for the legs, arms, chest, face, and birds. Cut the shims to the size and shape of each section. Attach the cut pieces to the shims with light-duty double-sided carpet tape.

SCARECROW: SHAPING THE PIECES

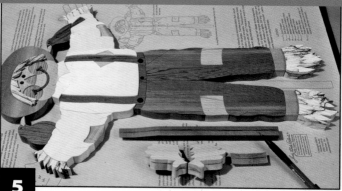

5 **Reduce the lowest pieces.** Reduce the thickness of the post, hands, and top of the hat to about ⅜" thick. Remove the wood from the top of the parts to keep everything square. The post is behind the legs and the hands are behind the straw.

6 **Shape the left crow.** Attach all of the crow parts except the beak to the sanding shim. Sand the crow down, removing about ⅜" of wood, until it appears to be sitting on the back side of the arm. Mark the area where the crow joins the sleeve.

7 **Shape the arms.** Round the straw so it appears to stick out from inside the cuffs. Sand the cuffs down to about ¹⁄₁₆" above the top of the straw. With the patches and the sleeves attached to a sanding shim, shape the sleeves. Round the edges down to the bottom except for the areas adjacent to the crows. Do not go lower than the mark indicating the thickness of the left crow, and do not over-round the area that meets the right crow.

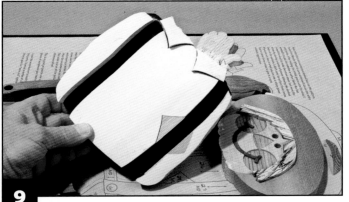

9 **Shape the right crow and collar.** Remove the sleeves from the sanding shims. Mark the right crow where it joins the sleeve. Sand the tail feathers and taper them toward the wing. The wing is thicker than the tail and the body. The body is thinner than the sleeve. Position the collar on the shirt sanding shim and mark the thickness of the shirt. Taper the collar in toward the face and round the outside edges as if it were following the scarecrow's neck.

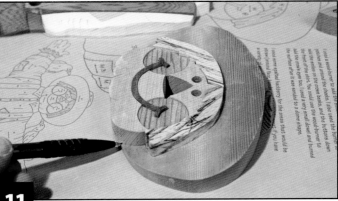

11 **Shape the brim of the hat.** Taper the hat down toward the chin. The upper brim at the front of the hat is the thickest part. You want to create the illusion of the back of the brim going behind the head. Mark the area where the chin joins the collar and the areas where the sanded hat joins the hair and face.

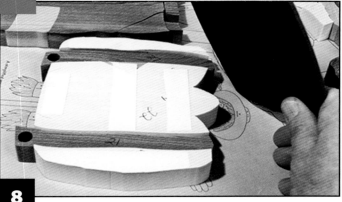

8 **Begin shaping the shirt.** Turn all of the shirt parts, including the suspenders, upside down and apply carpet tape to the white areas. Press the shim down over the inverted shirt. Hold the suspender pieces in place as you rough shape the shirt for a consistent contour. Remove enough wood to make the collar stick out. Remove the suspenders and remove ¹⁄₁₆" more wood from the shirt so the suspenders are thicker than the shirt.

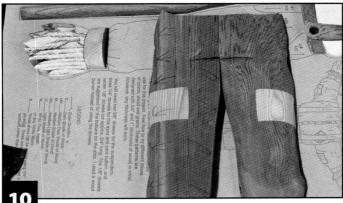

10 **Shape the pants.** Taper the straw down toward the cuff on the pant legs. Shape the cuffs and mark the pant legs where they pillow out from the cuffs. Securely tape each leg to a sanding shim. The patches follow the same contour as the pants. Round the pants toward the outside edges. Do not round the zipper area. The pockets are below the pants. The waistband is higher than the pants, but lower than the suspenders.

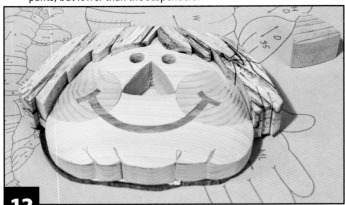

12 **Sand the face.** Shape the face as a unit. Attach all of the parts except the nose and eyes to a sanding shim. Keep the face thicker than the collar and add wrinkles at the neckline for a stuffed look. Mark the hair where it joins the face. Sand the hair thinner than the hat in the front, but thicker than the hat on the sides.

13 **Finish shaping the crows.** Mark the area where the beak meets the crow's face. Sand the beak down to this mark. Use a ⅛"-diameter walnut dowel for the crow's eye. Shape the beak for the second crow and add the eye. Darken the eyes with a woodburner.

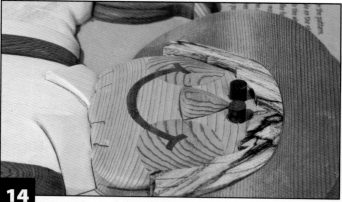

14 **Shape the nose and eyes.** Insert a ¼"-thick riser under the nose and mark the nose where it joins the face. Round from the center of the nose down the sides, stopping before the lines. Cut ¼"-diameter dowels for the eyes and sand them down to about 1⁄16" above the face.

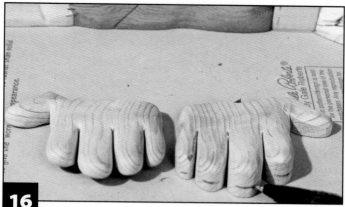

16 **Undercut the fingers and straw at the feet.** Sand the back of the fingers to make it look like the hands are pulling away from the backing board. Do not sand too much off the back. Leave at least two-thirds of the bottom flat. Remove just enough wood so the fingers cast a shadow on the backing board. Undercut the straw at the feet using the same technique.

TIP TRIMMING FOR FIT

If the cut parts do not line up with each other properly, you can often see where the piece is cut outside the pattern line. Trim these areas with a sharp blade. It is easier to keep the parts square by re-cutting rather than sanding up to the line.

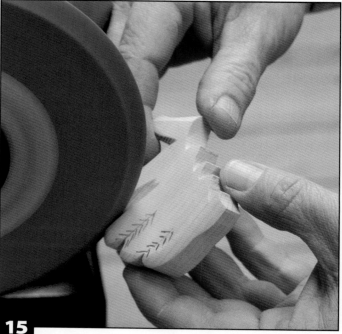

15 **Add the carved details.** Create definition between the fingers and add some wrinkles to the pants and shirt. I also add texture to all of the straw areas. I use a Wonder Wheel, but you could also use a carving knife, hobby knife, or rotary power carver. Soften the wrinkles in the clothing with sandpaper. Be careful using the Wonder Wheel; it can burn the wood if you are not careful.

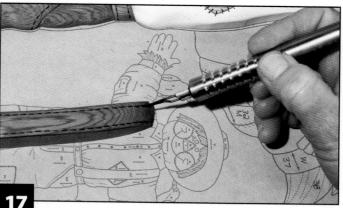

17 **Add the final details.** Take a final look at the assembled intarsia and refine any areas that need further shaping. Sand with the grain to clean up any scratches. Remove the dust and check for any remaining rough spots. I use a woodburner to add the stitching details and buttons and to detail the beaks on the crows. Practice on scrap wood to get a feel for the woodburner.

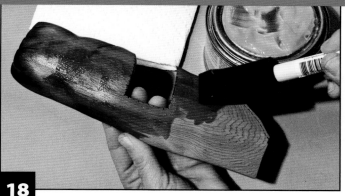

18 **Apply the finish.** Some parts of the face are fragile. Glue the face together before applying a finish. Apply the finish to the other pieces before assembly. I use gel polyurethane. Apply a heavy coat of the gel, wait a minute, and wipe away the excess. Do not apply finish to the back of the pieces. Allow the finish to dry overnight. Then apply two more coats, allowing each additional coat to dry for six to eight hours.

19 **Assemble the project.** Dry assemble the intarsia and trace the outline. Attach the traced pattern to hardboard and cut ¹⁄₁₆" inside the lines. Check the fit of the pieces on the backing board. I start by gluing three or four exterior pieces, such as the straw feet, the hands, the post, and the hat to the backing board. Allow the glue to dry and then attach the remaining parts. After the glue dries, attach a D-ring hanger to the back of the project.

TIP TRACKING THE BACKER BOARD

Apply a light coating of spray adhesive to a large sheet of paper. Then assemble the cut pieces on the paper. The light tack of the spray adhesive keeps the pieces from shifting as you trace around the intarsia to determine the shape of the backing board.

Materials & Tools

Materials:
- 5 copies of the pattern
- Glue stick or spray adhesive
- Double-sided light-traffic carpet tape
- Pencil
- ¾" x 6" x 10" dark wood such as dark western red cedar or walnut
- ¾" x 8" x 14" medium dark wood such as western red cedar, mahogany, or cherry
- ¾" x 6" x 12" medium wood such as western red cedar, pecan, or red oak
- ¾" x 6" x 8" medium light wood such as western red cedar, oak, or northern white cedar
- ¾" x 6" x 8" light wood such as western red cedar, hackberry, maple, or birch
- ¾" x 6" x 12" white wood such as aspen, white pine, or holly
- ³⁄₈"-diameter by 4"-long walnut dowel (buttons on suspenders)
- ¼"-diameter by 4"-long walnut dowel (eyes and pants button)
- ¹⁄₈"-diameter by 4"-long walnut dowel (crows' eyes)
- Finish of choice, such as polyurethane gel
- ¹⁄₈" to ¼" x 18" x 22" hardboard or plywood (backing board)
- Assorted scraps of ¹⁄₈" to ¼"-thick hardboard or plywood (sanding shims)
- Woodworkers glue
- D-ring hanger

Tools:
- #5 and #0 reverse-tooth blades or blades of choice
- Wonder Wheel (see page 140), carving knife, hobby knife, or rotary power carver
- Drum sanders of choice
- Woodburner

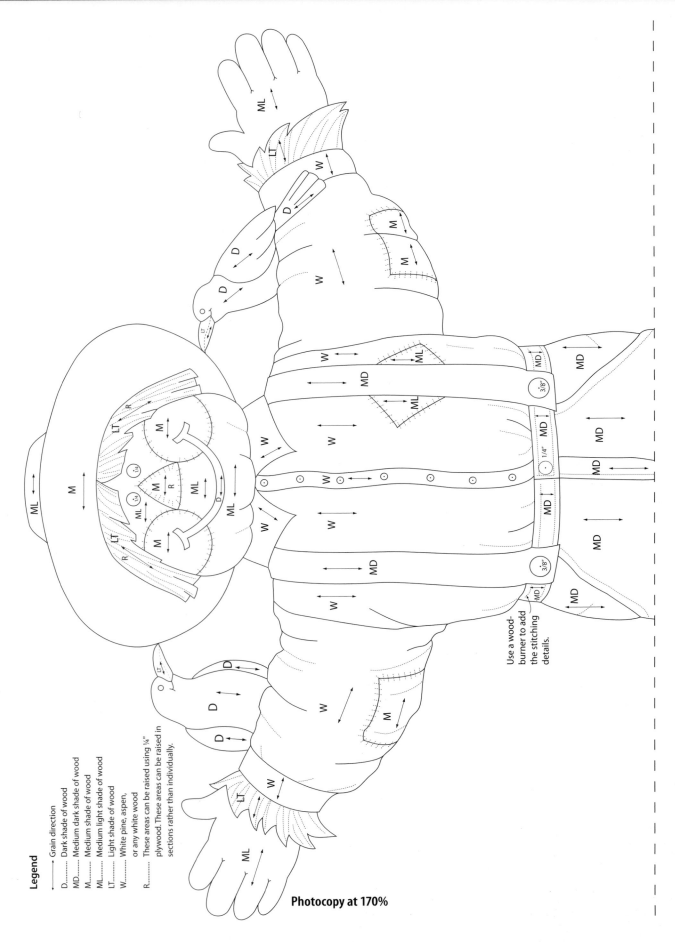

Legend

→ Grain direction

D.......... Dark shade of wood

MD........ Medium dark shade of wood

M.......... Medium shade of wood

ML........ Medium light shade of wood

LT.......... Light shade of wood

W.......... White pine, aspen, or any white wood

R.......... These areas can be raised using ¼" plywood. These areas can be raised in sections rather than individually.

Use a wood-burner to add the stitching details.

Photocopy at 170%

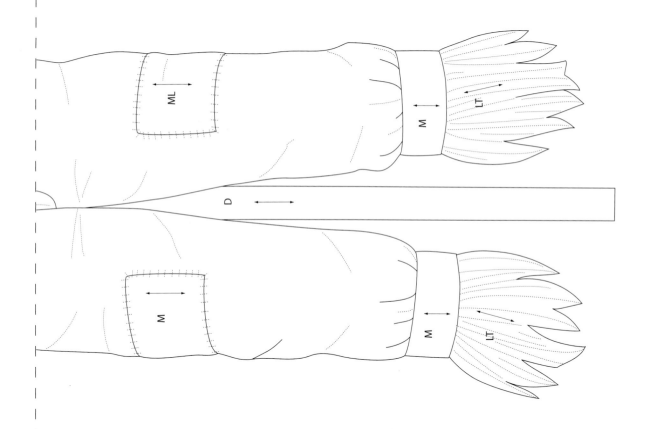

Photocopy at 170%

Cardinal Photo Frame

By Kathy Wise

This cardinal frame, in bright holiday colors, makes a great seasonal decoration. Use it to display the annual photo of the kid's visit with Santa or insert the latest family portrait for a cherished gift to grandma.

The bright cardinals and holly leaves, cut from bloodwood and elm, are glued onto a beech frame. Before you cut any pieces, make sure the bottom of the wood is flat. After you cut and shape the holly leaves and cardinals, glue them together with cyanoacrylate (CA) glue to make it easy to glue the subassemblies to the frame.

It is possible to cut the berries out of bloodwood, but I use dowels. Round one end of the dowel with a drum sander, then cut off the dowel at the correct length for each berry. After cutting and shaping the berries, stain or dye them red.

Cut the ¼"-thick backing board and spacer pieces to the sizes listed in the materials list. I use Masonite for these pieces because of its stability. Transfer the dotted lines on the pattern to the spacer piece and cut the opening.

Cut the beech frame pieces to size and cut a 45° miter on both ends of each piece. Apply wood glue to the miters and clamp the frame together until dry. Glue and clamp the spacer onto the back of the frame. The spacer will reinforce the miter joints. Then glue and clamp the backing board onto the spacer.

Materials & Tools

Materials:
- ¾" x 8" x 9" red wood such as bloodwood
- ¾" x 3" x 3" dark wood such as wenge
- ¾" x 2" x 2" medium light wood such as mandrone (beak)
- ½" to ¾" x 8" x 24" light wood such as elm (leaves)
- 2 each ½" x 2¼" x 14¼" medium-toned wood such as beech (long frame pieces)
- 2 each ½" x 2¼" x 11½" medium-toned wood such as beech (short frame pieces)
- 2 each ¼" x 11½" x 14¼" high-density fiberboard or plywood (spacer and backing board)

- ¼"-diameter x 6"-long dowel (holly berries, optional)
- Wood glue of choice
- Cyanoacrylate glue
- Red stain or dye (optional)
- Finish of choice (I use a satin spray varnish)

Tools:
- #7 reverse-tooth blades or blades of choice
- Miter saw or table saw (optional, easier to cut accurate miters)
- Assorted clamps
- Sander (I use a pneumatic drum sander)
- Sanding mop

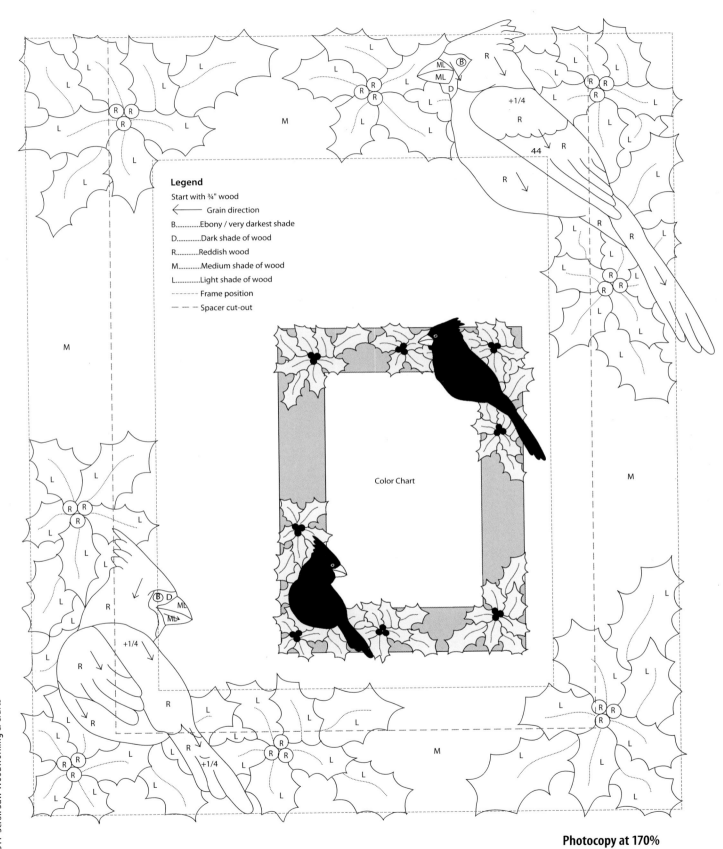

Legend

Start with ¾" wood

← Grain direction

B............Ebony / very darkest shade

D............Dark shade of wood

R............Reddish wood

M............Medium shade of wood

L............Light shade of wood

------ Frame position

— — Spacer cut-out

Color Chart

Photocopy at 170%

M

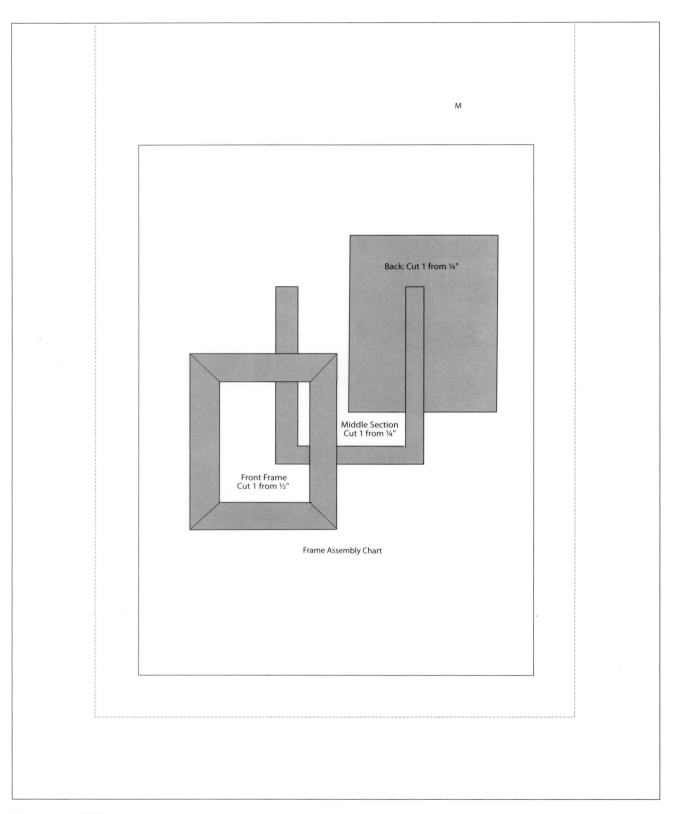

Back: Cut 1 from ¼"

Middle Section
Cut 1 from ¼"

Front Frame
Cut 1 from ½"

Frame Assembly Chart

Photocopy at 170%

Birds and Berries Winter Wreath

*By Kathy Wise and
Phil MacDonald*

Stylish cardinals, a goldfinch, a cedar waxwing, a chickadee, and a nuthatch adorn this intricate Christmas wreath, making it a wonderful gift for the backyard birder you know. Although this is a complex piece with many small pieces, you have the option of simplifying it to a much easier project if you desire. For more advanced woodcrafters, cut all 172 pieces. By cutting the solid lines on the patterns, beginners will cut only 106 pieces.

Though we have provided a list of woods we've used for the project, we encourage you to experiment with different woods. Doing so makes the piece truly your own.

Materials & Tools

Materials:
- ¾" x 10" x 4' medium brown western red cedar (M)
- 1" x 6" x 6" white basswood (W)
- 1" x 6" x 6" very dark walnut (D)
- 1" x 4" x 4" light basswood (L)
- 1" x 8" x 5" medium dark cedar (MD)
- 1" x 6" x 6" ash (G)
- 1" x 6" x 6" locust (Y)
- ¼" x 18" x 24" plywood for backer and risers
- ⅛" dowel

- 3⁄16" dowel
- Roll of clear shelf contact paper
- Temporary bond spray adhesive
- Yellow wood glue
- Gel natural varnish
- Wiping rags
- Sawtoothed hanger

Tools:
- #3 reverse-tooth blade
- Drill with ⅛"- and 3⁄16"-diameter bits
- Pneumatic-drum sander

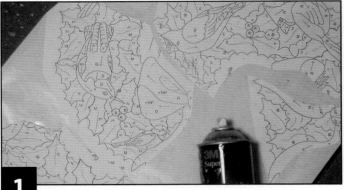

1 **Make about ten copies of the pattern.** Always keep a master copy to use later. Cut out and group pattern pieces together by color: dark, medium, light, and so on. Adhere color groups onto legal size paper with glue stick. Copy each set of color-sorted patterns; save a copy for future use. Tape contact paper flat on a board. Spray adhesive on the pattern and contact paper and put together. Cut out each paper pattern piece. Cut out the wreath in four large sections as indicated on the pattern.

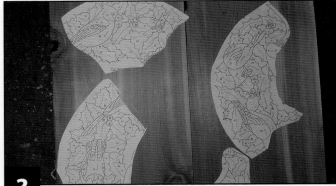

2 **Select your wood.** We used cedar for the wreath, but you can use any type of wood. Just keep in mind you want a medium to light shade so the birds and the bow will stand out. Try to get a fairly even grain with no great contrast between the grain stripes. You want the wreath to be a backdrop for the birds. Pick a good deep red color for the cardinal and the bow. Try to find a nice yellow for the goldfinch. There are some nice exotic woods to choose from. We used locust.
Your wreath will have more character and appeal with careful planning. Run the grain up and down on the entire wreath. Peel and stick pattern pieces on your selected pieces of wood lining up the grain direction.

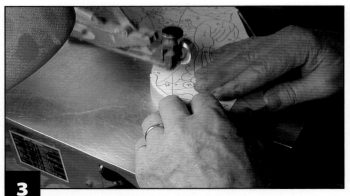

3 **I used a #3 blade to cut out this piece.** Make sure your blade is square to the saw table by using an angle to check a cut piece. Equally important is having flat wood for a good cut and fit. Plane any wood that is not flat. Cut out all four large ¾"-thick wood to allow you more freedom when shaping your wreath levels. Cut the outside lines with extra care on the two ends that meet the other part of the wreath pattern. If you are a beginner/intermediate, cut out only the 28 large sections of the wreath. If you are an advanced woodworker or would like a challenge, cut out each of the 94 wreath pieces, cutting out all the dotted lines. Cut the bird risers out of ¼" plywood as indicated in the pattern.

4 **As you get them done, lay out all the cut pieces on a full pattern taped to a work board.** Check for fit and make adjustments as needed. If you do not like the wood color or grain direction changes you see, change them now. On this piece, we decided we did not like the walnut in the dark area of the bow and recut the two pieces out of padauk to match the rest of the bow. Remember—the entire piece will darken with the finish.

TIP   **STOP SMALL PIECES FROM SLIPPING WHILE GLUING**

Gluing a lot of small pieces can be a nightmare. Hard-to-clamp areas or pieces sliding away from each other while gluing can be eliminated. I use a 100% silicone glue and tack each small area together. Have your entire project laid out on your backerboard. Use just a small dot in one or two places to glue together sections. Be careful not to place any glue where it will be seen or use so much that it will press up into your seams. Let dry overnight. We break up the project into five or six manageable pieces, depending on the complexity. When we press the entire project back together, the glued sections will be in the correct position for permanent gluing with yellow wood glue. Put sandbags on top of the glued project working from the outside edge to inside, instead of clamping. The 100% silicone glue (or caulk) works very well because it holds the pieces together nicely, will bend slightly, and is easy to remove in case you have to take apart a section for a better fit.

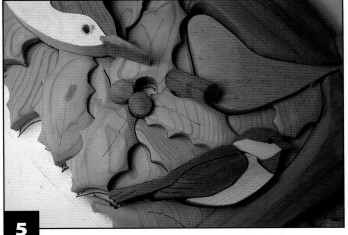

5 **I did all the roughing in of the varying depths by sanding and shaping with a pneumatic sanding drum.** Use a pencil to mark the depths you want on the sides of each piece. Using this as a guide, remove wood down to your line. Return each piece often to the pattern and next to the other leaves, this will make it easier to adjust to a pleasing level. This is where intarsia becomes a true art form. The woodcrafter's skill in sanding the pieces to varying levels gives a realistic three-dimensional feel to the finished piece. Don't be afraid to experiment. You can always recut another piece to take its place. Make sure, however, you have extra wood in each color.

6 **Refer to the shaping guide to help with finding your levels for the wreath.** Shape the leaves at a slanting angle with the high point being the tip of the leaf. Full leaves are the highest. Odd-shaped filler pieces are the lowest. Leaves are lower next to the birds and bow to make those higher pieces pop out. Slightly round all edges on each leaf, so you don't lose the sharp-edge look of real holly. Cut out your backer board using ¼" plywood. Use a full pattern and cut inside ¹⁄₁₆" around the entire exterior and inside hole. Any trimming of overhanging edges can be done with a sanding tool after the pieces are glued to the backer board.

7 **If you want to add a lot more depth and shape to your wreath, use a small ½" drum sander to carve a slight groove inside each holly leaf.** We used 120-grit sanding band and finished with a 240-grit sanding disk. Clean out line with a razor blade or carving knife.

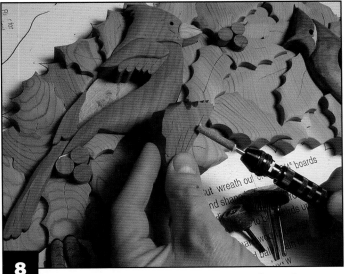

8 **Glue the small parts of the birds together for easier shaping.** We used a few different tools to carve the feathers in the wings and tails. Your tool choice will depend on the hardness or softness of the wood and personal preference. Experiment on scrap pieces to get the effect you want. Drill eyeholes with a ³⁄₁₆"-diameter bit for the nuthatch and waxwing and with a ⅛"-diameter bit for the other birds. Round off and burn the end of a dowel to make it black. Insert in correct holes and glue. This should be the last step before varnishing the birds.

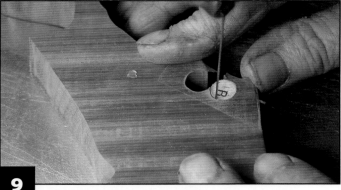

9 **Make the berries out of the same red wood as the bow and birds.** Put pattern on as a group of three, then cut apart each berry. Mark your berries' levels in relationship to the surrounding leaves. They should just rise above the leaves without sticking out too far. Shape into rounded tops using a sanding drum.

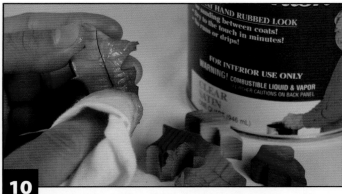

10 **Using a soft rag, hand wipe natural gel varnish on all dark and medium pieces, carefully covering the top and all side edges.** Apply one coat of white tinting on the white pieces to keep the wood from turning yellow. Let dry overnight, then put two coats of natural gel varnish on each piece. Let dry overnight before gluing. On the red bow and cardinals I used padauk. Padauk is a beautiful red wood, but it will darken greatly over time when varnished. A woodturner who works with padauk suggested using wax to seal the color. Apply on a polishing wheel and then use a small polishing wheel to get into all the cracks and fine carving areas. It has worked fine for me, but you may want to consider other red woods that are easier to finish and will not darken with age.

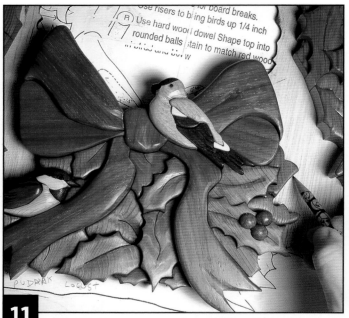

11 **Tack sections of wreath together with 100% silicone glue.** Tack the birds together and glue to risers, taking care to follow the pattern closely and have the riser inside the shape of each bird. Arrange and glue pieces to backerboard using wood glue. Let dry overnight. Because of the many pieces in this wreath, we glued the section with the two birds and bow first. Lay out all the pieces in the wreath on the backerboard and make sure you have a tight fit. Ease the pieces away from the section you are gluing and mark the edges with a pencil. Glue the first section down and weight with sandbags, working from the outside to the inside. The tacked section will remain together, making it much easier to glue. Let dry overnight. Now you can lay out the two sides of the wreath and mark the same as the first piece. Tack together and glue. On the last top section, if you have a problem with any gaps, simply pull apart the silicone-tacked sections of the leaves and space evenly to hide the open areas. Weigh down with sandbags and let dry overnight.

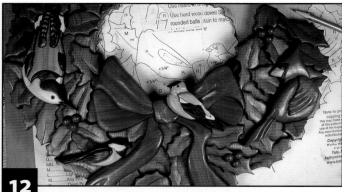

12 **Trim any overhanging backer board with a sanding drum and touch up stained edges.** Apply a final wipe of gel varnish on the entire piece by first saturating your wiping rag and wringing out. Use a light rub to wipe the varnish on the wood. Don't get a lot on the piece or you will have to spend time cleaning out the cracks. Attach a sawtoothed hanger and your festive Christmas bird wreath project is finished and ready for the holidays. We hope you enjoyed this challenging project!

Shaping Guide

Darkest gray is the
lowest level

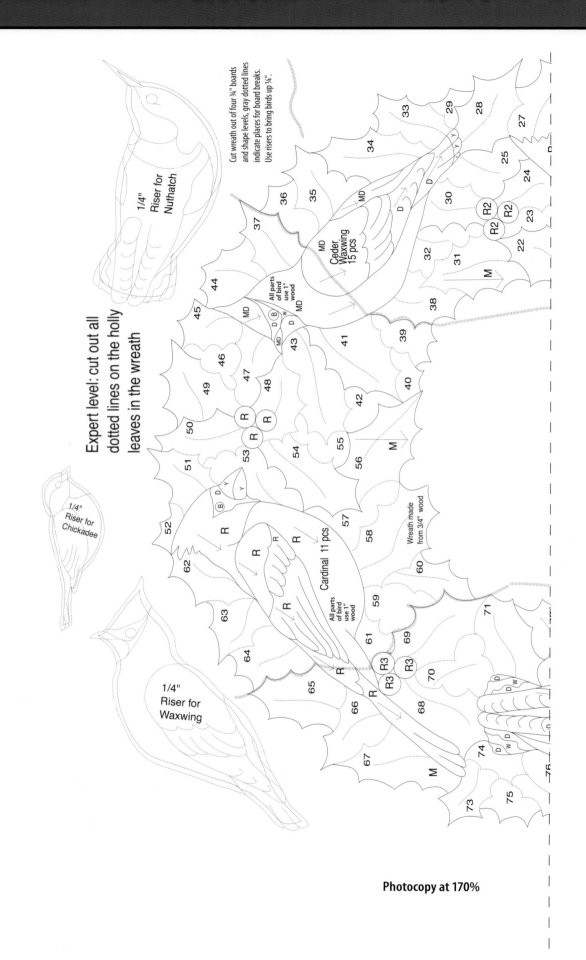

Expert level: cut out all
dotted lines on the holly
leaves in the wreath

1/4"
Riser for
Nuthatch

1/4"
Riser for
Chickadee

1/4"
Riser for
Waxwing

Cut wreath out of four ¾" boards
and shape levels, gray dotted lines
indicate places for board breaks.
Use risers to bring birds up ¼".

Ceder
Waxwing
15 pcs

All parts
of bird
use 1"
wood

Cardinal 11 pcs

All parts
of bird
use 1"
wood

Wreath made
from 3/4" wood

Photocopy at 170%

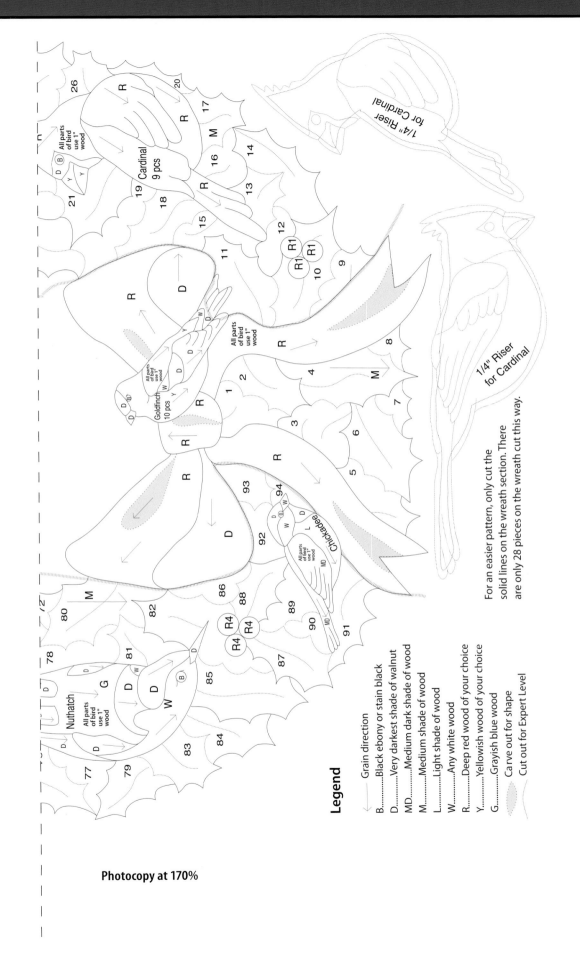

All parts of bird use 1" wood

26

R

20

17

R

M

16

14

13

R

Cardinal 9 pcs

19

18

15

12

R1

R1

R1

11

R

D

10

9

R

8

1

2

4

M

7

All parts of bird use 1" wood

All parts of bird use 1" wood

Goldfinch 10 pcs

W

Y

D

R

R

R

R

3

6

5

R

93

94

W

92

Chickadee

D

D

All parts of bird use 1" wood

MD

1/4" Riser for Cardinal

1/4" Riser for Cardinal

For an easier pattern, only cut the solid lines on the wreath section. There are only 28 pieces on the wreath cut this way.

21

D

B

Y

Y

80

M

78

82

86

88

R4

R4

R4

R4

89

90

91

MD

87

Nuthatch

All parts of bird use 1" wood

77

79

81

G

D

D

W

D

B

85

W

83

84

Legend

$\longrightarrow$ ...... Grain direction

B .... Black ebony or stain black

D .... Very darkest shade of walnut

MD ...... Medium dark shade of wood

M .... Medium shade of wood

L .... Light shade of wood

W .... Any white wood

R .... Deep red wood of your choice

Y .... Yellowish wood of your choice

G .... Grayish blue wood

.... Carve out for shape

.... Cut out for Expert Level

Photocopy at 170%

Animals

From the familiar puppy to the exotic toucan, this chapter gives you a wide selection of animal projects to choose from.

If it's winged things that capture your imagination, there is a chickadee, woodpecker, pelican, flamingo, and songbird.

Drawn to animals you might own or see in your backyard? Check out the squirrel, cat, raccoon, fox, colt, and pony.

And if what you really like is a reminder of the animal kingdom's majesty, take a look at the elephant, bobcat, and Arabian horse.

No matter which you choose, you can be sure your new pet will win lots of friends.

Brown Pelican Intarsia, by James West, page 166.

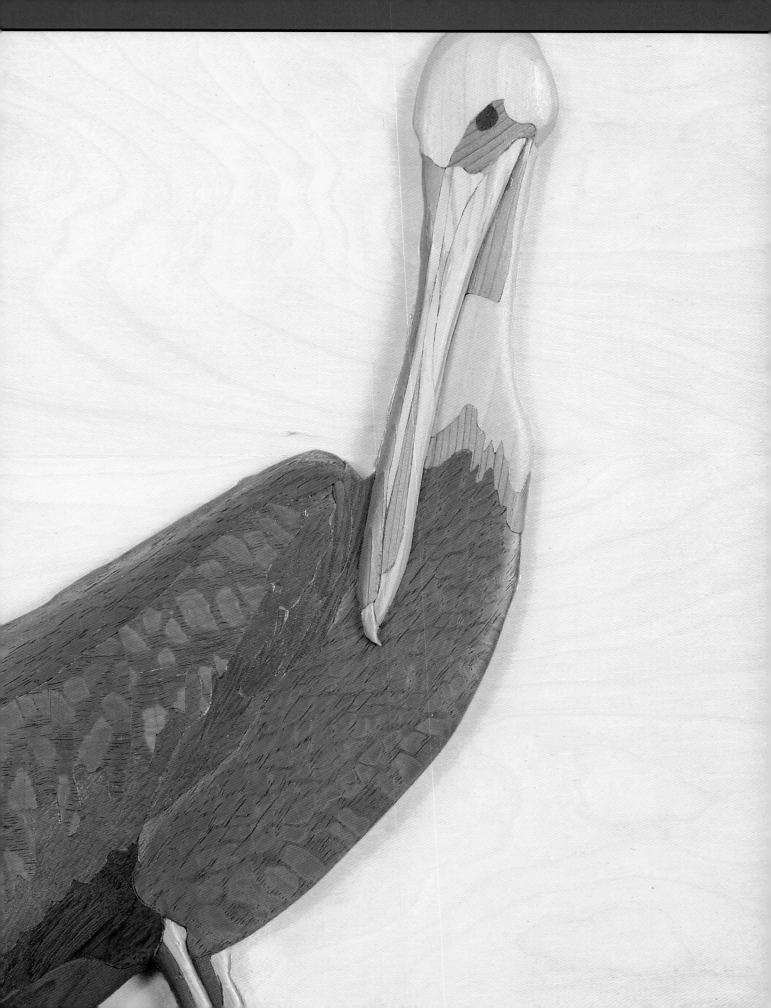

Intarsia Puppy in a Basket

By Judy Gale Roberts and Jerry Booher

You don't have to be a dog lover to fall in love with this cute Jack Russell terrier puppy nestled snugly in his western red cedar basket.

Jack Russells originated in England and are characterized mostly by white with black and tan markings. They are loyal stablemates for horses and great around children.

The "Jack" in this pattern is indeed looking for a good home and a loving family. What's more, you'll find him a cheerful and devoted companion to your many scrolled collectibles.

Step 1: Select the wood and prepare the pattern. The Jack Russell puppy and basket need four different shades of wood to achieve a rich multidimensional effect. As shown in the photo, ¾" western red cedar was used for the different shades and aspen for the white areas. You'll need two ⅜" dowels approximately ¾" long for the eyes; we used walnut dowels in this project.

Almost any type of wood will work, but the main guidelines for this project are color and grain direction. The following are alternative woods that will work nicely: walnut for the dark sections; cherry, mahogany, or pecan for the medium shades; oak or maple for the medium-light sections; and aspen, holly, poplar, or pine for the white shades.

Make at least five copies of the pattern at 100% to make one project because you will be cutting up the pattern parts and gluing them to the wood faces. Keep one pattern as your "master," and number all the parts on this pattern. Write the same number from your master onto each of the individual paper pattern pieces.

Step 2: Select a blade and begin cutting. We used a #5 reverse-skip-tooth blade for this project. The reverse teeth on the blade cut on the up stroke, which helps to decrease the tearout on the bottom of the piece.

If you use the same color board to lay out many parts, start by rough cutting them into smaller, more manageable sections.

Cut up each piece of the pattern that has a different color or grain direction. On the ML parts of the basket, the W portions of the dog's face, and the M parts of the basket's interior, the pattern parts can be cut in one section. As long as the color and grain direction are the same, you can leave these sections together. When cutting a part it's best to position the center of the blade in the center of the layout line, thus removing all of the line.

Leave about ¼" around the pattern's exterior when cutting. We generally scroll all the white sections first, then the dark, and so on. Cutting hand-sized pieces with several parts laid out on them is much easier to manage than one large board.

Start by sawing the easiest parts first. While sawing, stop often to remove the tearout. Always try to have a plan in mind when starting to cut a part so you don't end up with a very small part you are trying to hold. Make your cuts so the last piece will drop from the larger block.

The speed we use depends on the material(s) being cut. The main thing to remember is control. Intarsia requires accurate cutting, so you might want to experiment with your saw's speed to achieve the best control. We usually run about 60 to 70% of the speed range on our variable-speed saw.

Lastly, after cutting the pieces, turn them over and deburr the bottoms to remove any residual tearout. This procedure ensures the wood sits flat on the table.

Step 3: Check for fit. When all of the parts are cut and deburred, print the same number on the bottom as you have on top. Do not remove the pattern at this point. Then, assemble the parts and check to see how they fit. Leaving the paper on helps you spot fitting problems resulting from cutting outside of the pattern line.

Step 4: Making shims for sanding and raised portions. The main pattern shows the raised sections marked with an R and provides drawings for these pieces. Cut these pieces out of ¼" plywood and slide them under the raised parts.

While cutting out shims, we also make sanding shims, which helps sand areas in sections rather than individually. This practice makes for a more consistent contour of all the parts. On this dog, we make a sanding shim for the face, neck, and body portions.

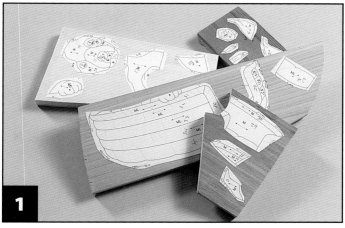

When selecting wood for the puppy in a basket, varying shades of western red cedar work best. But feel free to experiment with different color variations of walnut, cherry, mahogany, pecan, oak, maple, aspen, holly, or pine.

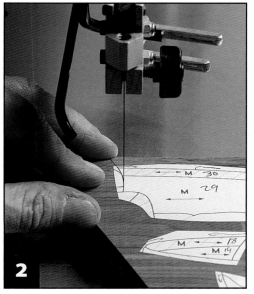

Place the center of the blade in the center of the layout line to remove all of the pattern line.

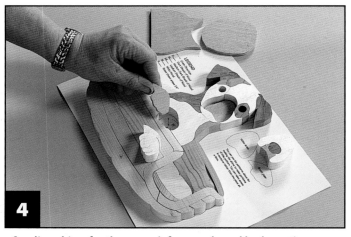

Sanding shims for the puppy's face, neck, and body sections make for more consistent contours.

By lowering parts farthest from the viewer, such as the interior portion of the basket, you create a more dimensional appearance. The thickness of this section is reduced by half by sanding.

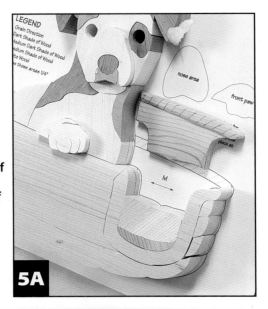

5A

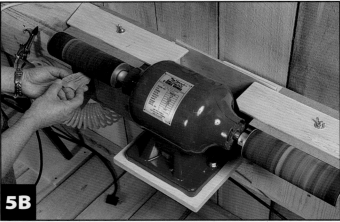

5B

While flexible-drum sanders make smoother contours, sections can be shaped with a deburring tool, flexible-shaft grinder, wood rasp, or 1" belt sander. Or, the project can be left flat with softened edges.

After each part is sanded, mark the piece with a mechanical pencil where it joins other parts.

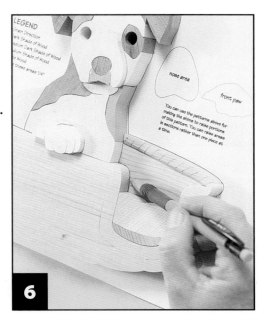

6

Step 5: Lower the background parts. It's best to rough in the entire project first, then come back and fine tune each part. We start with the parts that would be the farthest from the viewer. By lowering some parts and raising others, the project will start to look more dimensional. On this pattern, the back (or interior portion) of the basket would be the farthest from the viewer. Sand this part first, removing at least half the thickness of the wood.

We use a flexible-drum sander, one drum with 80-grit and the other with 120-grit. This tool, shown in Step 5B, makes it easier to achieve softer contours. However, other tools and methods can be used to create the same finish. Regardless, remove most of the material with 80-grit sandpaper, and then smooth it out with 120 grit.

Step 6: Mark adjoining pieces. After you sand each part, mark the piece with a mechanical pencil where it joins other parts. These lines will be your guides. As you work your way up to the thicker areas the parts will have lines all the way around them. Try not to sand below the pencil line. If you do accidentally sand below the line in this case, for instance, sand the rear of the basket lower.

Step 7: Keep marking. Sand the back portion of the dog. Mark the chest area, and sand it just above your pencil lines. Use double-sided tape to tape the chest areas together. Put the tape on the backs of the parts, then peel off the paper, and stick the plywood to the back. This way you can sand the entire section together. Take the sanding shim off, and mark around the dog's paw. Stay above your pencil line as you sand.

Mark around the dog's paw, and stay above your pencil line when you sand.

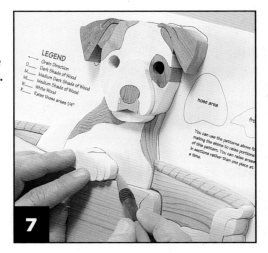

7

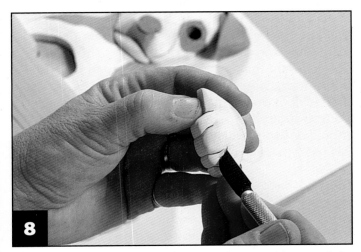

8

After rounding the paw, carve between the toes with a rounded hobby knife to give them a more lifelike appearance. The nostrils can be carved in this manner too.

9

Use double-sided tape and a sanding shim for the puppy's face.

Step 8: Carve the details. After the paw has been rounded, go back and carve between the toes to give them more definition. We use a rounded blade, but use whatever tools you have.

Step 9: Use double-sided tape. Use a sanding shim for the face section. Take the eyes and the nose out before applying the double-sided tape because you'll sand these parts later. When taping the face to the shim, be sure to add the raising shim to the back of the nose. Tape the shim along with the other face pieces to the sanding shim.

Step 10: Blend the nose and head. With all the parts together, blend the upper nose area with the forehead. You can also round the upper portion of the head toward the outer edge at this time. Remove the nose section and sand the lower portion of the face. Insert the nose, and mark where the face meets the nose. Sand the outer edges of the nose, making sure to stay above your pencil line.

Step 11: Sand the ears and pillow. After blending the face section, remove it from the sanding shim. Next, mark where the face joins the ears. Sand the inner ear portion down to your pencil line; then, mark where it joins the ear's outer flap portion. Sand the outer flap portion, leaving the point on the end the thickest and taper it down toward the top of the ear. Sand the pillow portion. Watch your pencil lines to keep from sanding the pillow thinner than the back of the basket.

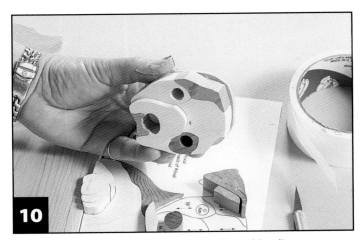

10

Assemble the nose and head sections prior to blending.

After removing the blended face section from the sanding shim, use a pencil to mark where the face joins the ears.

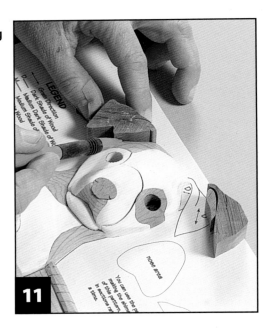

11

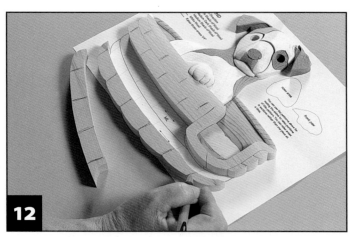

The dashed dips in the basket section of the pattern create an alternating weave effect.

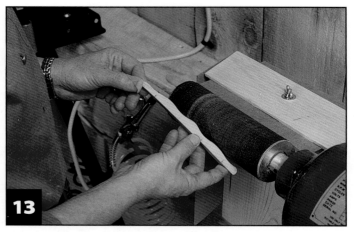

The basket's dips can be contoured using a 2½", or smaller, drum on a flexible-drum sander. However, the dips can be carved or scrolled too.

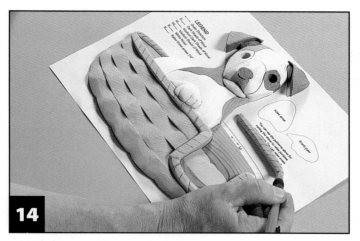

Mark the weave lines on the basket's rim.

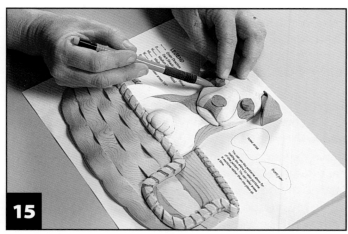

Sand the eyes slightly below the pencil line because the eyes will be a little thinner than the area around them.

Step 12: Weave the basket. Use the pattern to mark the dips that give the basket a weave effect. Sand the basket by rounding the outer edges and tapering down toward the bottom edge. Then, mark along the bottom edge and on the face of the wood, using the dashed lines on the pattern as a guide. Marking the bottom edge will enable you to see where the dip should be after sanding the face of the wood. You will need to make sure the dips alternate.

Step 13: Sand the dips. Place the drum directly across the line to create the dip. The photo shows a 2½" drum, which is about the largest diameter you can use to sand the dips. A larger width does not achieve the same affect. You also can carve these sections or perhaps turn the piece on its side and scroll the dips with your saw.

Step 14: Mark the rim's weave lines. Mark the weave lines using the same technique as above for marking the dips. We used a graphite-impregnated Wonder Wheel to make the grooves. It carves and burnishes the wood all in one stroke. These details can also be carved, gouged, or burned.

Step 15: Finish the eyes and nose. When shaping the eyes, sand them slightly below the pencil line because the eyes will be a little thinner than the area around them. Highlight the eye by gluing and inserting a small dowel-like piece of aspen into a small drilled hole. When the glue dries, sand it flush with the rest of the eye.

Mark around the outside edges of the nose and round the nose over to the point where the edge is sanded down to your pencil marks. The nose will be the thickest part on this project. If it's not thicker, raise it up using either a ⅛" or ¼" shim. For added detail, carve the nostrils using the dashed lines on the pattern as a guide.

Step 16: Apply the finish. There are many finishes and techniques that can be used, so feel free to use your favorite method.

We like to apply the finish to each part before gluing the project down. We use a wiping gel applied with a 1" disposable foam brush. Apply a heavy first coat and let it set for less than one minute. Wipe off the excess with a paper towel and buff it completely dry using a clean paper towel. After all parts have the first coat, let them dry for at least six to eight hours. Apply the second coat in the same manner and let it set for another six to eight hours.

Before the third and final coat, dress the "white" wood sections lightly with steel wool. Skip the cedar: gel does not raise its grain as it does on white woods. Apply and wipe the third and final coat of gel, letting these coats dry for at least four hours before going to the final step.

Step 17: Trace the finished project to make the backing. We use white paper with a light dusting of spray adhesive to keep the parts from moving. Use spray adhesive to apply the tracing to a piece of ¼" or ⅛" plywood. Cut a little to the inside of the line. We stain the edges dark and spray the back with a clear acrylic to seal the entire project.

We use yellow wood glue and a little hot-melt glue to affix the piece to the backing. Putting the hot-melt glue on the lower basket ring and the two ears prevents shifting until the wood glue dries.

When gluing the piece to the backing, make sure the pieces are aligned correctly. Glue a few outer pieces to lock in the entire project.

A little glue goes along way; there is no need to flood the glue on the back of the parts. Just a few dots across the back of each part will suffice.

Last but not least, find a centerpoint on the back and place your hanger. We use a mirror hanger.

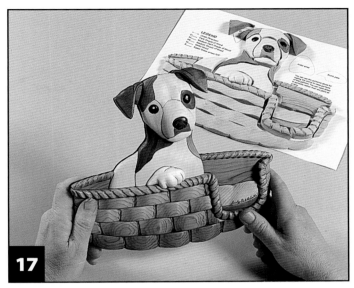

Before and after finishing. The finished, mounted project is in the foreground, with the unfinished piece in the background.

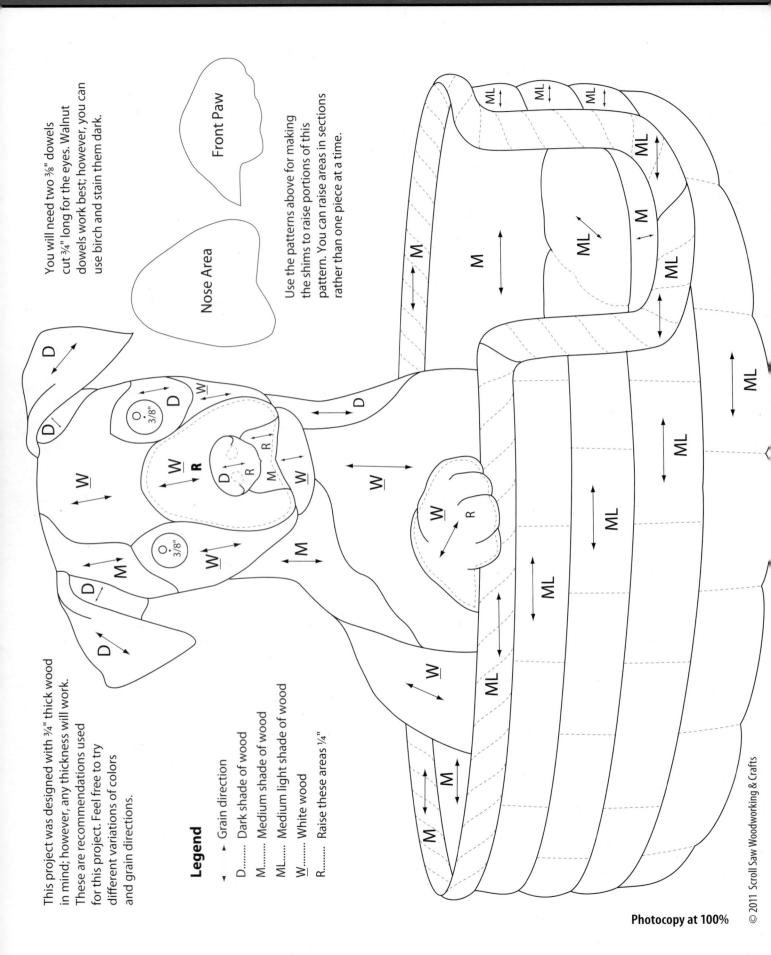

This project was designed with ¾" thick wood in mind; however, any thickness will work. These are recommendations used for this project. Feel free to try different variations of colors and grain directions.

Legend

► Grain direction

D.......... Dark shade of wood

M.......... Medium shade of wood

ML........ Medium light shade of wood

W.......... White wood

R........... Raise these areas ¼"

You will need two ⅜" dowels cut ¾" long for the eyes. Walnut dowels work best; however, you can use birch and stain them dark.

Front Paw

Nose Area

Use the patterns above for making the shims to raise portions of this pattern. You can raise areas in sections rather than one piece at a time.

Photocopy at 100%

Making Easy Intarsia Magnets

By Janette Square

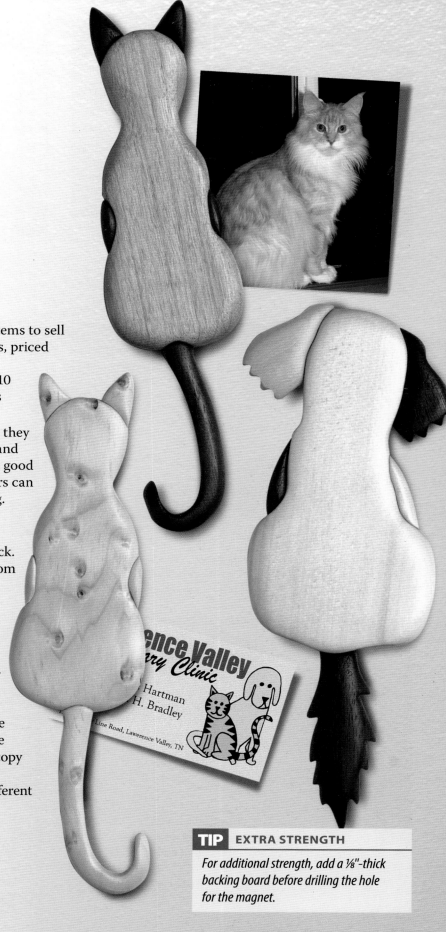

I'm always trying to come up with inexpensive items to sell at arts and crafts shows. My small intarsia pieces, priced between $25 and $40, have always been very popular. I designed these magnets to be in the $10 to $15 price range. The magnets make great gifts and are fun to display.

The best part about these magnets is how easy they are to make. Each magnet consists of six pieces and requires minimal shaping. Beginners can expect good results on their first try, and experienced scrollers can quickly build an inventory for sales or gift giving.

The magnets are an ideal way to use up wood scraps. You can create two magnets at once by cutting the shapes from stock that is ¾" to 1" thick. Then slice the shapes in half to get two pieces from each one. Beginners, or those without access to a band saw, may want to use thinner wood to avoid cutting the pieces in half. You can also stack cut several pieces of thin stock to create multiple magnets.

I use bird's-eye pine and butternut for the solid-color magnets. Peruvian walnut is paired with alder or aspen for the two-color designs. Cover the wood with clear packaging tape and attach the patterns to the tape with spray adhesive. If you are making a solid-color magnet, you only need one copy of the pattern. If you are using contrasting wood, make two copies of the pattern and attach the different pattern sections to the appropriate stock.

TIP EXTRA STRENGTH

For additional strength, add a ⅛"-thick backing board before drilling the hole for the magnet.

MAGNETS: CREATING THE INTARSIA

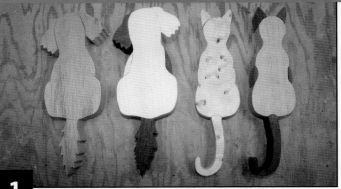

1 **Cut the pieces.** If you are cutting the magnets from a single piece of wood, you do not have to be as cautious about cutting exactly on the lines. If you plan to cut the pieces from two different colors of wood, the closer you stay to the line, the better the pieces will fit together.

2 **Slice the pieces in half.** This step is necessary only if you are using thick wood. Use a ruler to mark the center of one piece across its thickness. Use this mark to set the guide on the band saw. Use a holding block to cut each piece in half, producing two identical pieces. Resaw the smaller pieces in half with a scroll saw.

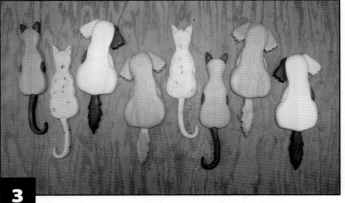

3 **Shape the pieces as desired.** Be careful when holding the small pieces. Use a 180-grit sanding drum and then a 220-grit sanding drum. Buff the pieces with a mop sander and hand sand any areas requiring extra attention. Dry assemble the pieces to check for fit and then glue the pieces together with wood glue.

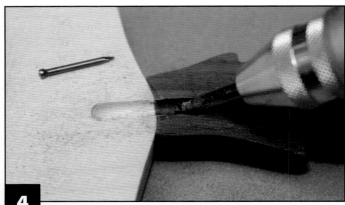

4 **Reinforce the tail.** Carve a small groove across the joint of the tail and the body with a rotary power carver. Make the groove slightly deeper than the thickness of the brad. Fill the groove with wood filler or epoxy and push the brad into the material. Let the filler dry and sand it smooth.

MAGNETS: ATTACHING THE MAGNET

5 **Drill the hole for the magnet.** Chuck a ¼"-diameter Forstner bit in a drill press and set the drill press to drill a hole ½ the thickness of the magnet. Test the fit of the magnet in the hole. Set the magnet aside and apply your clear finish of choice. Let the intarsia pieces dry overnight.

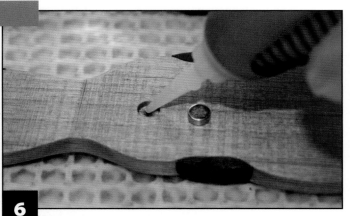

6 **Attach the magnet.** Place the intarsia face down on wax paper. Carefully apply cyanoacrylate (CA) glue gel to the hole and place the magnet over the glue. Wear latex gloves and use a wood skewer or dowel, not your fingers, to push the magnet down until the glue dries. Remember to sign the back of the magnet.

Pet Magnet Patterns

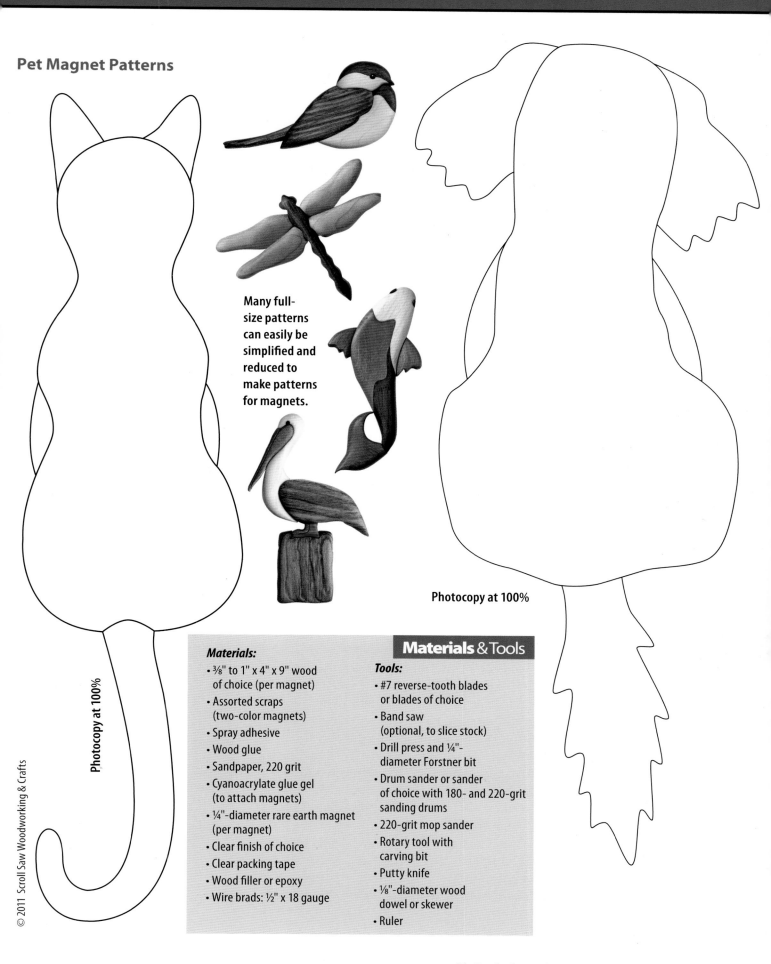

Many full-size patterns can easily be simplified and reduced to make patterns for magnets.

Photocopy at 100%

Photocopy at 100%

Photocopy at 100%

Materials & Tools

Materials:
- ⅜" to 1" x 4" x 9" wood of choice (per magnet)
- Assorted scraps (two-color magnets)
- Spray adhesive
- Wood glue
- Sandpaper, 220 grit
- Cyanoacrylate glue gel (to attach magnets)
- ¼"-diameter rare earth magnet (per magnet)
- Clear finish of choice
- Clear packing tape
- Wood filler or epoxy
- Wire brads: ½" x 18 gauge

Tools:
- #7 reverse-tooth blades or blades of choice
- Band saw (optional, to slice stock)
- Drill press and ¼"-diameter Forstner bit
- Drum sander or sander of choice with 180- and 220-grit sanding drums
- 220-grit mop sander
- Rotary tool with carving bit
- Putty knife
- ⅛"-diameter wood dowel or skewer
- Ruler

Kid-Friendly Toucan

By John Morgan

Although many scrollers learned woodworking basics in shop class, today's youth depend, for the most part, on family and friends to pass along those skills. I remember watching in amazement as a toy box, cabinets, toolboxes, stilts, bean flips (slingshots), and my wooden skateboard came to life at the hands of my father. He encouraged me to participate whenever possible. The earliest project that I remember was the "screwdriver holder" that I hastily cut, drilled, then glued and screwed to the side of my father's workbench (and he never complained). Working with my dad was fun—the way it should be!

My main goal here isn't to teach you how to create a segmentation project, but to encourage you to share your love of woodworking with the children in your life.

My boys, Zach and Aaron, have always loved to "build" with their dad. When they were small, I kept a box of scraps in the corner of the garage so they could work beside me. More often than not, they ended up in the wood shavings and sawdust.

Now 11 and 8, they enjoy drilling holes, helping dad fire the nailgun, and using the scroll saw. I don't push woodworking on my sons. They come out and watch when they want, and go in when they are through. I never run them off when they just show up to see what's going on, unless I'm spraying something, or there is a lot of fine dust, and I can't get them some protection.

If they ask to help, I try to find something for them to do, such as using the air compressor to dust off parts that have been cut, wiping pieces down with tack cloth, or testing the fit of pieces that have to go together.

I also suggest projects for us to do together. I let them choose the ones they like, which peaks their interest and keeps them wanting to do more. When they make an obvious mistake, we learn and go on. And, most important, I let them do as much of the work as safely possible. During each project, I let them do as much as they feel comfortable with. Nothing is more rewarding than their big smiles and sense of accomplishment and pride when the project is completed.

I wish to dedicate this project to my dad, James Morgan, for sharing his love and knowledge of wood and tools, as well as his patience and guidance.

Cutting

I let Zach and Aaron cut most of the project. Older kids can cut the pieces on their own, but younger children may require a little help. I still stand right over my younger son, often times with my hands on his, or his on mine, to get a "feel" for the cutting operations. I cut the tricky parts, like the circle around the eye, the black portions of the beak, and the tiny talons. Then I cut the ¼"-thick plywood backing board for the assembled project to be glued to.

Preparation

I typically transfer the design and cut the perimeter of the pattern, or at least cut it down to a manageable size. I find tracing the pattern onto the wood is easier because the boys don't have to worry about the paper pattern lifting up as they are cutting. I let Aaron drill the hole for the dowel eye.

Sanding

We pre-sand the board before gluing on the pattern and cutting the segments. The boys use folded pieces of sandpaper and small sanding sticks to round the edges of each piece and to remove any fuzz on the backside. I cut the dowel for the eye to length, but the boys shaped the piece. Aaron sanded the wrong side of a few pieces, so I showed him how to tell which side needed sanding, and on he went. You can put a mark on the back of the piece to avoid any confusion. We then put our pieces back together on top of an extra copy of the pattern, to make sure that all pieces had been sanded and the edges rounded over. I also showed them how to remove the sanding dust with an air compressor or tack cloth.

Painting

Be sure to cover your workspace with newspaper before beginning. The boys use

common craft paints to color the segments. I showed them, on some pieces, that paint didn't need to cover all of the sides. I then let them try to figure out which of the remaining segments should be painted the same way, or fully covered. A few were painted that didn't need to be, and some had to be painted more upon final inspection. Some were painted with a thin coat, and some looked like they had been dipped! Remember, the mistakes are teachable moments! You can show them a picture of the completed project to follow my paint scheme, or let them create their own. It doesn't matter if the project accurately represents the colors of a toucan—just that they have fun doing it.

Final Assembly

With the potential of this getting messy, I pointed out where glue needed to be spread. The boys took turns brushing on glue and placing each piece back together (they assembled the toucan on a sheet of wax paper). Once dry, the boys brushed glue on the backer board and placed the assembled toucan on the backer board. Zach applied pressure for a few

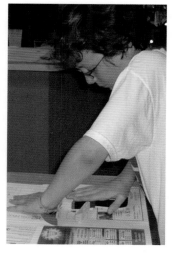

minutes to make sure it was set. I sprayed the project with several coats of clear spray and nailed a sawtoothed hanger to the back. It's important to have them help clean up after the project is finished.

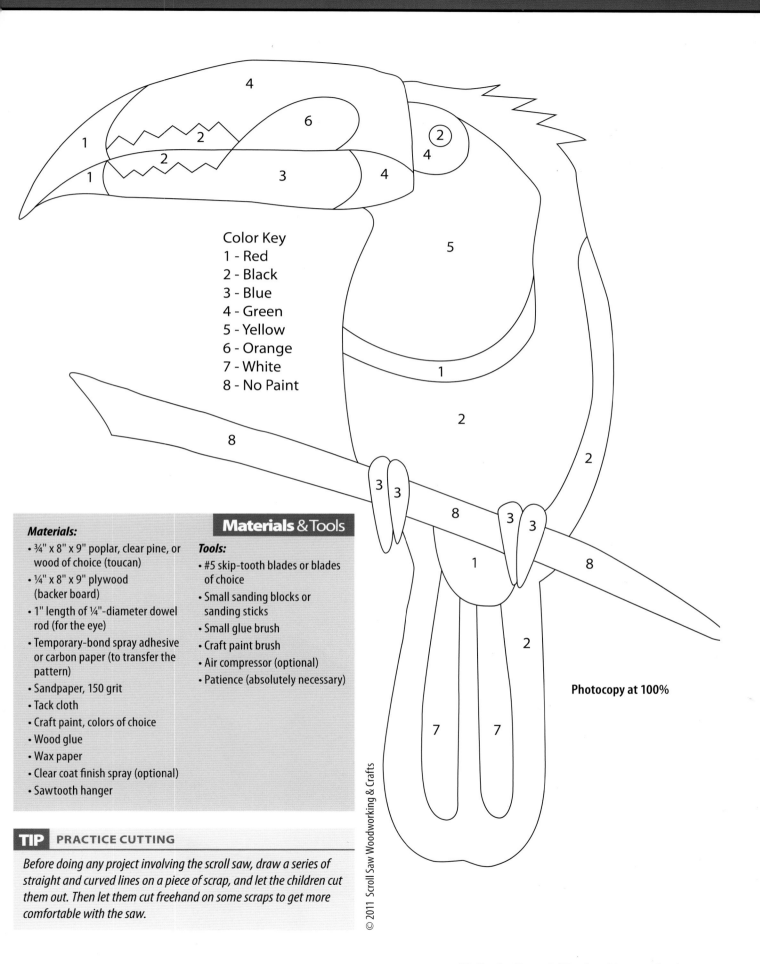

Color Key
1 - Red
2 - Black
3 - Blue
4 - Green
5 - Yellow
6 - Orange
7 - White
8 - No Paint

Photocopy at 100%

Materials & Tools

Materials:
- ¾" x 8" x 9" poplar, clear pine, or wood of choice (toucan)
- ¼" x 8" x 9" plywood (backer board)
- 1" length of ¼"-diameter dowel rod (for the eye)
- Temporary-bond spray adhesive or carbon paper (to transfer the pattern)
- Sandpaper, 150 grit
- Tack cloth
- Craft paint, colors of choice
- Wood glue
- Wax paper
- Clear coat finish spray (optional)
- Sawtooth hanger

Tools:
- #5 skip-tooth blades or blades of choice
- Small sanding blocks or sanding sticks
- Small glue brush
- Craft paint brush
- Air compressor (optional)
- Patience (absolutely necessary)

TIP PRACTICE CUTTING

Before doing any project involving the scroll saw, draw a series of straight and curved lines on a piece of scrap, and let the children cut them out. Then let them cut freehand on some scraps to get more comfortable with the saw.

Springtime Chickadee

By Janette Square

This intarsia design is based on an original acrylic painting by Cindy Kobriger.

I love to watch the chickadees at our birdfeeders, flying everywhere with their distinctive chirps. This intarsia piece is a year-round reminder of their cheerful presence. Because the piece is not too large or labor intensive, I can price the completed project economically, making it a great seller at art shows.

Last spring, I did an arts and crafts show in Florence, on the Oregon coast. I met Cindy Kobriger, who sold original acrylic paintings on note cards. I purchased Cindy's beautiful chickadee painting. Cindy graciously gave me permission to create an intarsia design based on the painting.

This chickadee is not a difficult project, yet it still presents a reasonable challenge. Use ¾"-thick wood for the majority of the design. Use 1"-thick wood for the leaves so you can taper the bottom of the chickadee to make it appear behind the leaf. I use green poplar for the leaves. Substitute a red or orange wood, such as padauk, for autumn leaves.

Materials & Tools

Materials:
- ¾" x 4" x 6" light wood, such as white sycamore, aspen, or birch (belly, head, eye)
- ¾" x 3" x 4" red wood, such as red sycamore or cherry (breast, beak)
- ¾" x 3" x 4" grey wood, such as blue pine (feathers)
- ¾" x 3" x 4" dark wood, such as Peruvian walnut or black walnut (head, eye, back)
- ¾" x 4" x 6" dark-grained wood, such as bocote (branch)
- 1" x 6" x 7" green wood, such as poplar (leaves)
- ⅛" x 8½" x 11" Baltic birch plywood (backing board)
- Clear packaging tape
- Temporary-bond spray adhesive
- Antique white acrylic paint (eye highlight)
- Sandpaper, 220 grit
- Hanger of choice
- Wood glue
- Permanent markers (for signing and coloring edges of backer)
- Clear satin gel varnish or finish of choice

Tools:
- #5 or #7 reverse-tooth blades or blades of choice
- Sanding tools (flex drum, oscillating spindle sander, mop sander)
- Clamps (to hold backer in place until glue dries)
- Skewer (to apply highlight dot to the eye)
- Glue brush
- Dental tools and air compressor (to remove finish from crevices)
- Disposable foam brush

Legend
P......Peruvian walnut
D.....Dark wood
G.....Green (poplar)
B......Blue pine
A.....Aspen
R......Red sycamore

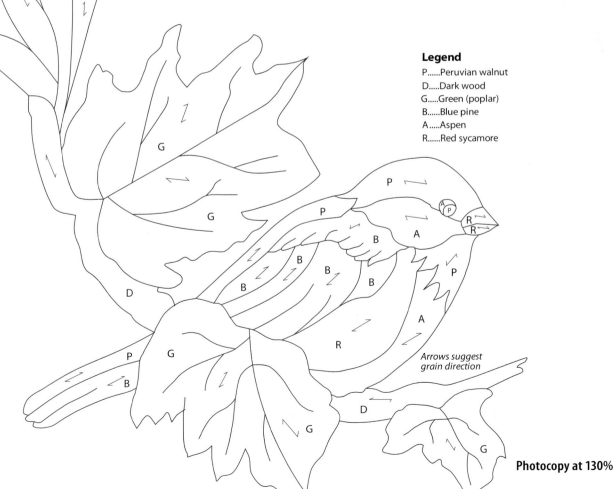

Arrows suggest grain direction

Photocopy at 130%

© 2011 Scroll Saw Woodworking & Crafts

Big Book of Intarsia Woodworking—Animals 123

Toucan Mosaic Trinket Box

By Diana Thompson

Designing mosaics to accent boxes is one of my favorite techniques. The box itself is made of sassafras—a wood I've not used before. Since it seemed lightweight, I thought it might be a good wood for cutting things that are a bit thicker, such as the box sides in this pattern. I've since tried cutting 1½" thick wood for some of my compound patterns, and it's great. The wood resembles ash in texture and color but cuts much easier. And if you like root beer, this is the wood for you. That's what my shop smells like when I'm working with this wood.

At one time, root beer was made from the roots of this tree—it may still be.

Sassafras can cause respiratory problems and nausea in certain individuals. You should always wear a dust mask and be careful when working with this wood.

Start by applying the patterns to the individual pieces with spray adhesive. Match the patterns to the stock by following the directions printed on the patterns and in the materials list.

1 **Cut the box side.** Drill a blade-entry hole and cut the inside line on the box side pattern. Do not remove the pattern. Glue the underside of the box side to one piece of the ¼"-thick wood. Clamp and allow to dry for at least an hour. Use as many clamps as you need to get a tight joint.

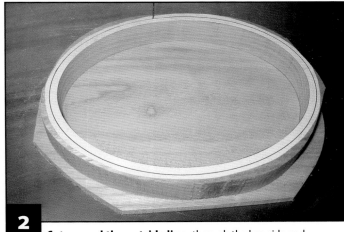

2 **Cut around the outside line,** through the box side and the ¼"-thick box bottom. Then use a disc sander to smooth the edges of the box. Be careful to keep the piece moving, or you will end up with flat spots. This method can be used for the lid pieces as well.

3 **Round over the bottom of the box with the ⅛" radius roundover bit.** Remove the pattern, and sand the box smooth with 400-grit sandpaper. Cut out the backing board and the lid underside according to the directions on the pattern. Do not remove the lid underside pattern.

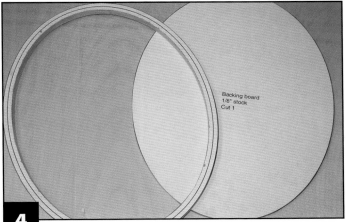

4 **Apply glue to the lid underside, and glue it to one side of the backing board.** Clamp securely and allow it to dry. While it's drying, cut the lid frame and segmentation.

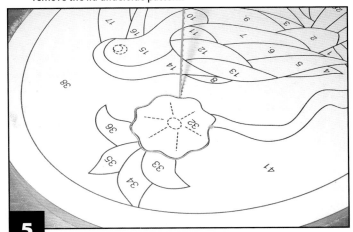

5 **Drill a blade-entry hole in the lid upperside, using as small a bit as possible.** Cut around the outside of the lid upperside. Thread the blade through the blade-entry hole and begin cutting the mosaic design. Do not cut the dashed lines; they are for detail painting. I use a #5 reverse-tooth blade to make room for the paint. If the wood will be left natural, use a #3 reverse-tooth blade for a closer fit.

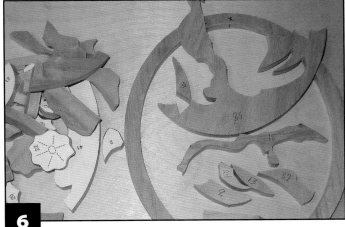

6 **Transfer the number of each piece to the back side before removing the pattern.** Also mark the back side of the lid upperside frame before removing the pattern. A paper or plastic bowl is handy for keeping all the pieces together in one place. I don't recommend using a glass or ceramic container in the shop, due to breakage.

7 **Round over the inside of the lid frame as you did for the box bottom in Step 3.** Apply glue to the underside of the frame, and glue it to the other side of the backing board. The backing board should be sandwiched between the lid underside and lid upperside frame. Use as many clamps as necessary to get a tight fit. When dry, cut around the center line of the lid underside. Round over the upper and lower outside edges as you did in Step 3.

TIP **ROUTER SAFETY**

Attach a piece of clear acrylic with a ½"-diameter hole cut in the center to the top of your router table. With this closer tolerance to the bit, it makes it easier to round over the small pieces. The acrylic can be held to the table with a few pieces of double-sided tape or a shot of spray adhesive.

10 **Paint the mosaic pieces with acrylic craft paints.** Painting the side of the pieces once is usually enough. I add an extra coat on the top of the surface to ensure good coverage. Use my color scheme or your own imagination. The eye is done with a black pen. I left the box natural because I like the combination of natural and paint, but you could paint it. When the paint is dry, arrange the pieces inside the frame, but do not glue them down.

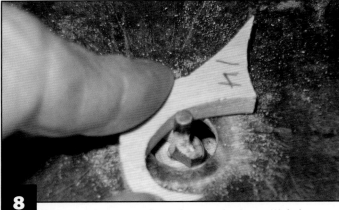

8 **Remove the pattern from the mosaic pieces.** With the numbered side facing up, round over the edges. Pay particular attention while doing this step; your fingers will be very close to the sharp router bit, particularly for the smaller pieces. You can also use 150-grit sandpaper to round over the smaller pieces by hand.

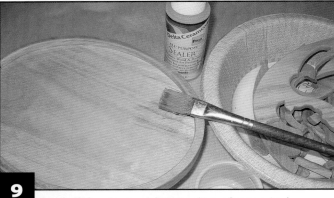

9 **Sand all the pieces with 400-grit sandpaper.** Apply a wood sealer, allow it to dry, and sand it smooth again. I use a water-based sealer, which is easy to clean up and widely available at craft stores. To avoid unwanted wood movement, also seal the underside of the mosaic pieces.

11 **Place a board over the lid, and turn it upside down.** Remove the frame and apply wood glue to the backing board. Replace the frame back onto the mosaic pieces. Turn it right-side up and adjust mosaic pieces as needed while the glue is still wet. If the mosaic pieces stick up a bit, clamp a board over it until it's dry. Apply several coats of clear finish.

Materials & Tools

Materials:
- ¾" to 1¼" x 7½" x 5½" wood of choice (box side)
- ¼" x 8" x 6" wood of choice (box bottom)
- 2 each ¼" x 6" x 7½" wood of choice (lid upper and lower liner)
- ⅛" x 6" x 7½" wood of choice (lid backing piece)
- Wood glue
- Sandpaper 150, 220, & 400 grits
- Spray adhesive
- Pencil

Finishing Supplies:
- Assorted small brushes
- Wood sealer

- Clear spray finish of choice
- Black pen
- Craft paints of choice. I used the following:
  Licorice (feathers)
  Lemon chiffon (face)
  Sunny yellow (beak)
  Petal pink (blossoms)
  Caramel candy (tree branch)
  Wicker white (top of the tail feathers)
  Sky blue (sky)
  Bright red (little bit of tummy feather area)
  Wedgewood green (leaves)
  Hunter green (leaves)
  Bright magenta (blossom centers)

Tools:
- #5 reverse-tooth blades & #5 single-tooth blades (or blades of choice)
- Rotary tool with router table attachment
- ⅛"-radius roundover router bit (Make sure it's a round over bit and not a beading bit. They look very much alike!)
- Scissors
- Assorted small clamps
- Disc sander (optional)

TIP BABY WIPES

Keep a box of baby wipes in your shop to clean the glue from your hands and the project itself.

Lid upperside

¼" stock

Make two copies and use the outer line of the second one to cut the lid backer from ⅛" wood.

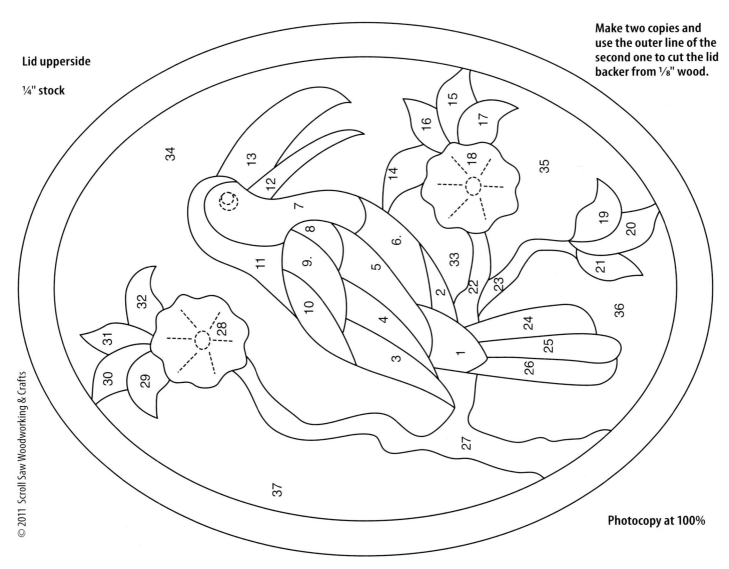

Photocopy at 100%

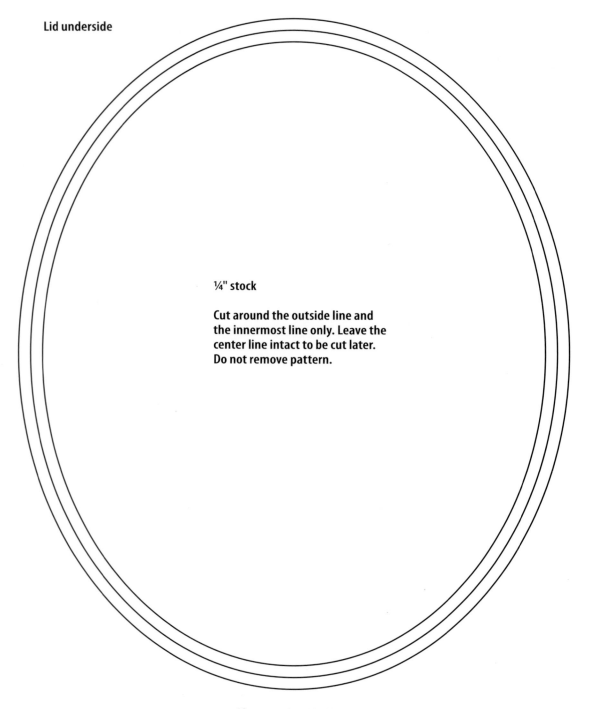

Lid underside

¼" stock

Cut around the outside line and
the innermost line only. Leave the
center line intact to be cut later.
Do not remove pattern.

Photocopy at 100%

Box sides

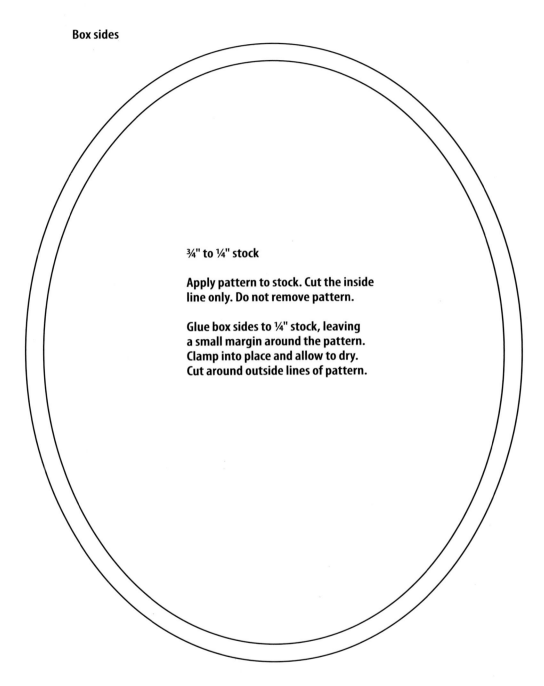

¾" to ¼" stock

Apply pattern to stock. Cut the inside
line only. Do not remove pattern.

Glue box sides to ¼" stock, leaving
a small margin around the pattern.
Clamp into place and allow to dry.
Cut around outside lines of pattern.

Photocopy at 100%

Squirrel

By Kathy Wise

This whimsical squirrel design is inspired by the crafty little rascals that are always raiding my bird feeder. I use red cedar for the main body sections and cut the white sections from poplar. The dark highlights are cut from black walnut and ebony is used for the eyes.

I finish all my pieces with a gel stain before they are glued together and glued onto the backing board.

Legend

Start with ¾" wood

← Grain direction

B.......Black ebony or
       very darkest shade

D.......Dark shade of wood

MD....Medium dark shade

M.......Medium red shade of wood

W.......Any white wood

-1/4....Sand or plane down ¼"

+1/4...Use ¼" thicker wood

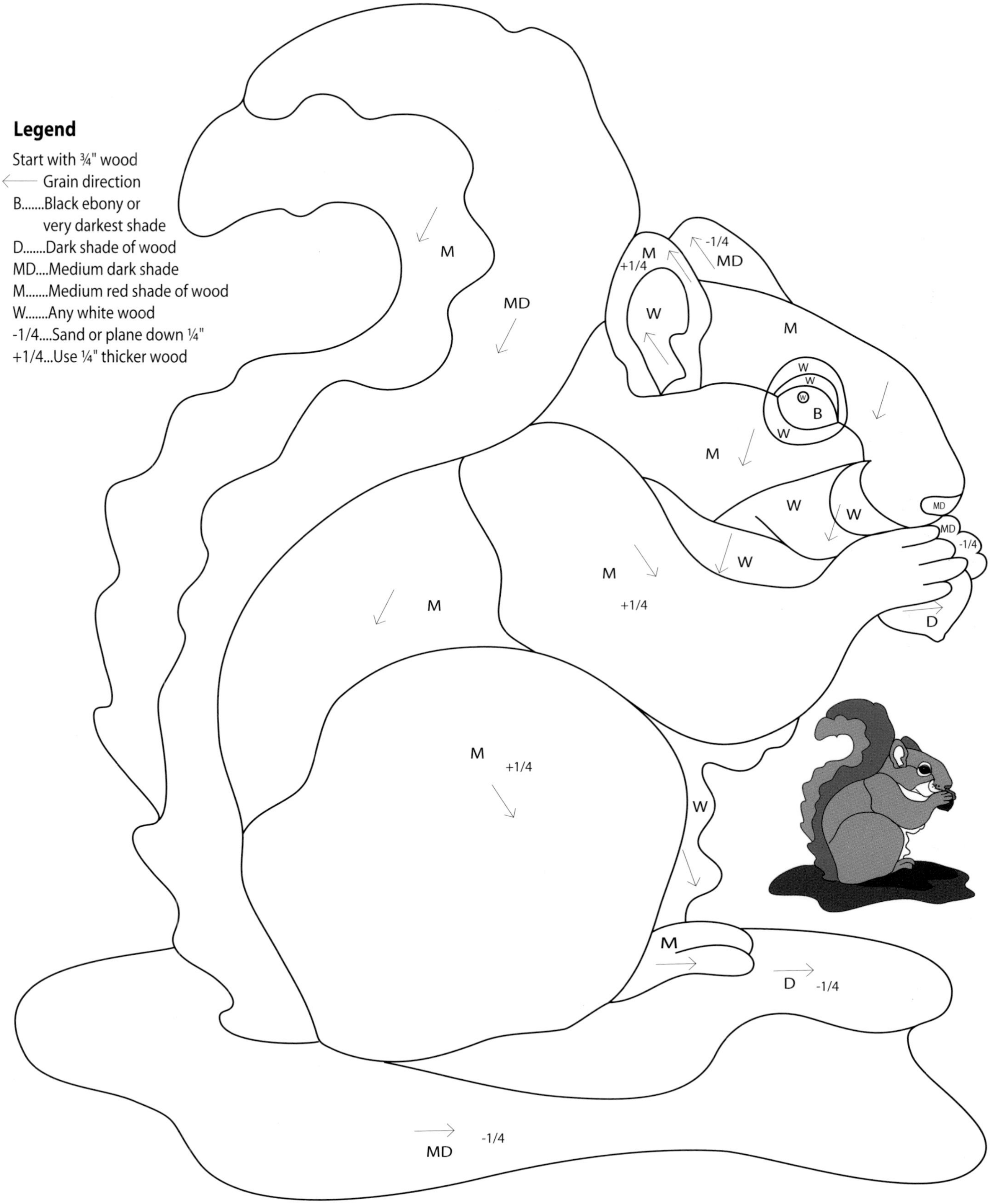

M

MD

M
+1/4

M

MD

M

W

W

W
W
W
B

W

W

M

W

W

M
+1/4

W

M
+1/4

M

M
+1/4

MD
+1/4

W

M

D
-1/4

MD
-1/4

D

MD
-1/4

Photocopy at 100%

Arabian Horse

By Kathy Wise

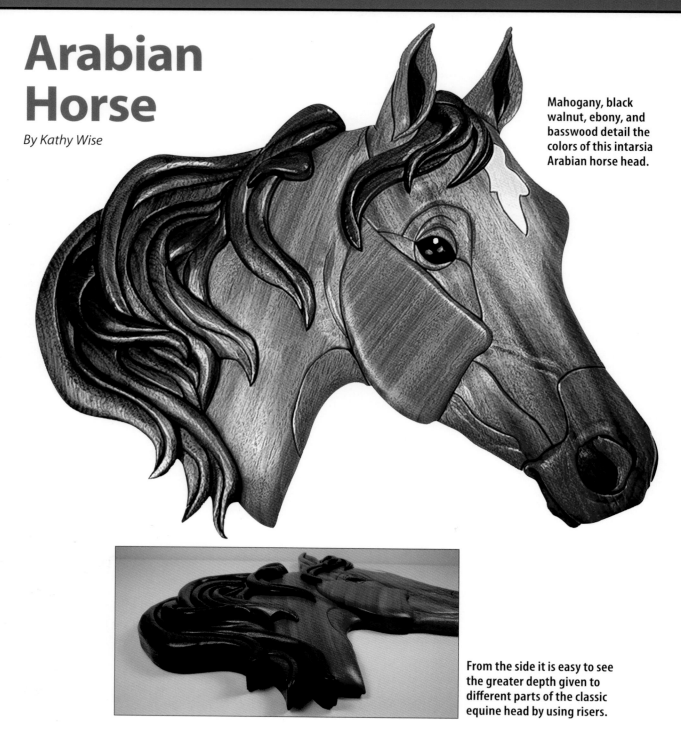

Mahogany, black walnut, ebony, and basswood detail the colors of this intarsia Arabian horse head.

From the side it is easy to see the greater depth given to different parts of the classic equine head by using risers.

Not only are Arabians some of the most beautiful horses to look at, they also are one of the toughest and most enduring breeds. For centuries, Arabian horses have been used to improve and refine other horse breeds around the world. Now you can memorialize one in intarsia!

Any number of wood species can be used to create this stunning intarsia horse. I used black walnut for the mane, mahogany for the bay color, ebony for the eye, and basswood for the blaze. Feel free to substitute different colored woods to make your work unique.

Although this mane was cut from several colors of walnut, you can simplify it by cutting it out of a single piece of wood and sanding in the varying levels of the mane to achieve the flowing lines. There is a little light carving on the nose to accent the nostrils and veins in the face. This pattern is designed for an intermediate to advanced woodcrafter.

Special thanks to my father-in-law, Phil MacDonald, for his help and advice with this project.

1 **Make about 10 copies of the pattern.** Always keep a master copy to use later. Cut out and group pattern pieces together by color: dark, medium, light, and so on. Attach the color groups onto legal-size paper with glue stick. Copy each set of color sorted patterns; save a copy for future projects. Tape the contact paper flat on a board. Spray adhesive on the pattern and put together. Cut out each paper pattern piece. Starting with totally flat wood, peel the backer off the contact paper and adhere the pattern piece to the wood lining up the grain direction.

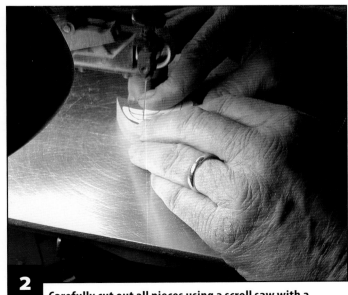

2 **Carefully cut out all pieces using a scroll saw with a #5 blade or your blade of choice.** Make sure your blade is square to the saw table by using a square to check a cut piece. Always mark the back of your piece. Lay out all your cut pieces on a pattern taped to a work board and check for fit.

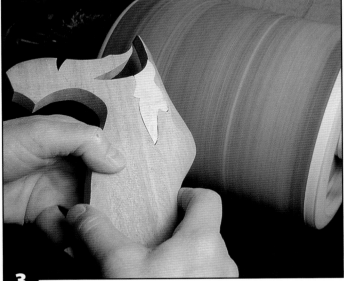

3 **Shape and sand each piece individually.** I use a pneumatic drum sander. Glue the basswood blaze into the horse's forehead to shape the pieces together. Use a pencil to mark where you want to take off excess wood. Replace pieces back into the project often to check how much wood you are removing, and re-mark as needed. You want to achieve depth and shadows in your mane.

4 **Lightly round the edges of each piece.** Use a rotary power carver with a ½" sanding drum to round the inside edges of the mane you can't reach with the pneumatic-drum sander. Cut ¼" shims for the two higher pieces of the mane.

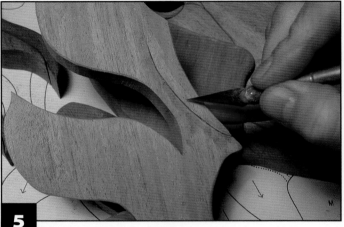

5 **Carve the under chin details.** I use a hobby knife, but a ¼" veiner gouge also works well. Follow the line on the pattern with the veiner to create a rounded wrinkle. The veiner cuts a deep enough groove to give the wrinkle depth, but also leaves the wrinkle rounded and natural looking.

6 **The wrinkles over the horse's eye were made with the ½" sanding drum and a carving knife.** Take your time carving and shaping this area, especially if you have never carved before. These features really bring the horse head to life. If you don't want to do any carving on this piece, simply cut the dotted lines in the middle of the face and shape. Then ignore the dotted areas around the nostrils and above the eye.

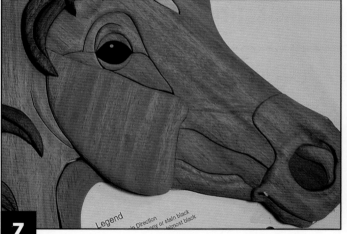

7 **You can use a flexible shaft tool with a small sanding drum to create the graduated curves in the nose area and the face.** Or you can use a ¼" veiner or a ⅜" gouge to carve the two veins in the face where shown on the pattern. Follow the dotted lines to add dimension to the lower part of the horse's face. Then use the flexible shaft tool to recess the area around the nose to help pop out the nostril and give the piece a more 3-D feel.

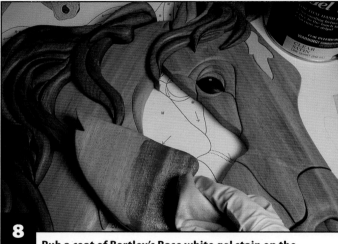

8 **Rub a coat of Bartley's Base white gel stain on the white wood of the blaze to keep it from turning yellow.** Take care not to get any on any other part of your horse. Let the stain dry overnight. Using a soft clean rag, apply clear gel varnish to all the pieces, carefully covering the top and all the side edges. Let it dry for a few minutes before wiping it off with a clean rag. After it's dry, apply a second coat and let it dry overnight. Cut the backer board out of ¼" plywood. Use the whole pattern but cut ¼" inside the outline. Mark the glue side with a marker. Stain the edges of the board dark mahogany. Sand the glue side and remove any stain that may have gotten on the face of the board to ensure clean and tight gluing.

TIP **MAKE YOUR OWN SANDBAG**

Fill resealable freezer bags with sand to make your own sandbags. Buy any grade of sand blasting sand, or use clean, screened beach sand to make your own sand bags for weighing down pieces while gluing. Be careful not to get sand into the seal part of the bag. Press all the air out of the bag and seal. Take a strip of duct tape, bend the end over and tape, taking care not to have any sharp edges. Put the sandbag into another bag and seal and tape the end. Cover the entire bag with duct tape. This will keep the plastic bags from puncturing and spilling sand all over your project and workshop. It will make it very durable and will not slip when you pile more than one or two sandbags on your project.

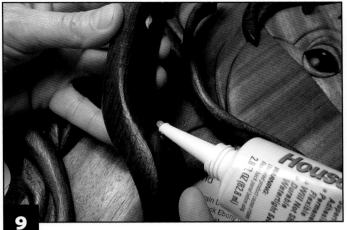

9 **Tack the sections of the horse together with 100% silicone glue.** Tack the small mane parts together and glue them to the risers, taking care to follow the pattern closely. Make sure the risers don't stick out beyond the sections of the mane.

10 **Tack other sections of the horse head with 100% silicone glue.** The tacked sections will remain together, making it much easier to glue. If you have any gaps, pull apart the silicone tacked sections and space them evenly to hide the open areas. I glue the mane section in four large pieces. I also tack the entire nose section and the eye/forehead section together. Let the glue dry overnight.

11 **Lay out all the tacked sections of the horse head on the backer board and make sure you have a tight fit.** Ease the pieces away from the section you are gluing and mark the edges with a pencil. Glue the first section down with yellow woodworking glue and weigh them down with sandbags, working from the outside to the inside. Let the glue set up for a couple hours. Then glue the rest of the horse head down and weigh down with sandbags again pressing them from the outside to the inside. Let the glue dry overnight.

12 **Trim any overhanging backer board with a rotary power carver and a sanding drum and touch up the edges with stain.** I like to put a final wipe of gel varnish on the entire piece at this point. Saturate your wiping rag and wring out—use just a light rub. Don't get a lot on the piece or you will have to spend time cleaning the excess out of the cracks. Then attach a sawtooth hanger.

Materials & Tools

Materials:
These are suggested types of wood; you can use your own wood of choice.
- 1" x 12" x16" dark walnut
- ¾" x 2" x 6" white basswood
- ¾" x 3" x 6" ebony or very dark walnut
- ¾" x 8" x 24" mahogany
- ¼" x 24" x 12" plywood for backer and risers
- Roll of clear shelf contact paper
- Spray adhesive
- Glue stick
- 100% silicone glue
- Yellow woodworking glue
- Gel natural varnish
- White base gel varnish
- Sawtooth hanger

Tools:
- #3 or #5 blade
- ³⁄₁₆"-diameter drill bit
- Pneumatic-drum sander
- Wiping rags
- Hobby knife or carving tools

Depth Guide

52 pieces

Photocopy at 145%

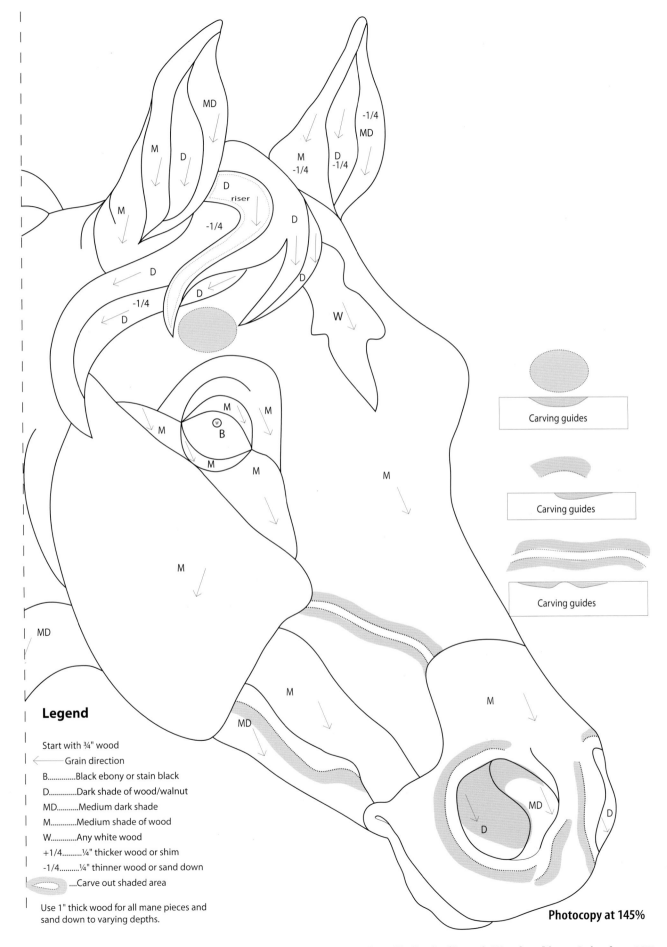

Carving guides

Carving guides

Carving guides

Legend

Start with ¾" wood

⟵ Grain direction

B.............Black ebony or stain black

D.............Dark shade of wood/walnut

MD..........Medium dark shade

M.............Medium shade of wood

W.............Any white wood

+1/4..........¼" thicker wood or shim

-1/4..........¼" thinner wood or sand down

⬭ ....Carve out shaded area

Use 1" thick wood for all mane pieces and sand down to varying depths.

riser

Photocopy at 145%

Pileated Woodpecker

By Judy Gale Roberts

The *Pileated Woodpecker* was inspired by my love of nature. I used red heart for the crest and added texture to the tree, which is a great way to break up all the smooth pieces of wood. Using different techniques to add texture creates contrast in intarsia projects. Watching the wood come to life as you sand and shape it keeps intarsia fun for me. After 30 years of creating intarsia pieces, I still get excited when the grain works out perfectly.

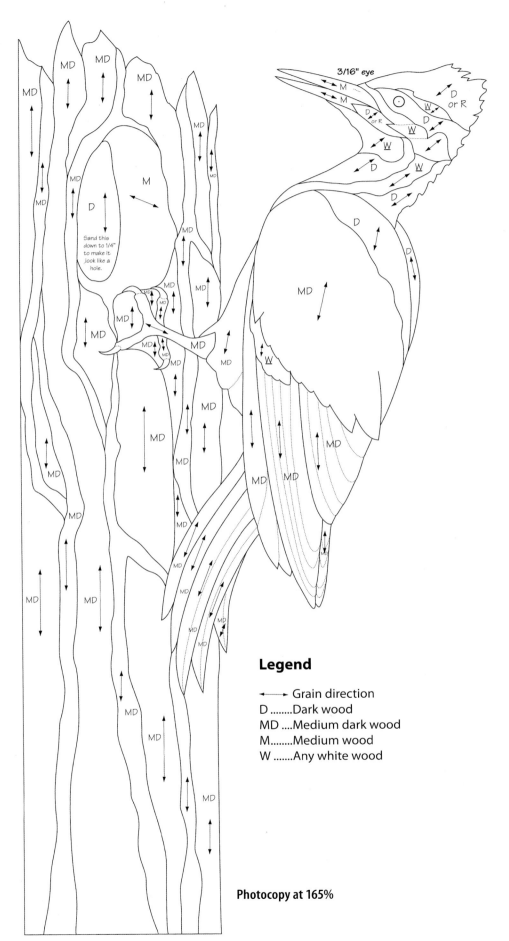

Legend

→ Grain direction
D ....Dark wood
MD ....Medium dark wood
M........Medium wood
W ....Any white wood

Photocopy at 165%

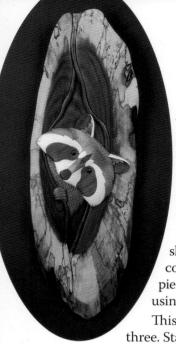

Raccoon Intarsia

By Judy Gale Roberts and Jerry Booher

Adding texture to your animal intarsia piece is guaranteed to make it stand out in a crowd. Intarsia authorities Judy Gale Roberts and Jerry Booher developed an easy way to add fur texture and highlights to your wildlife intarsia.

Judy and Jerry walk you through shaping intarsia pieces so they "flow" correctly, elevating and lowering pieces to give the intarsia relief, and using tools to suggest texture.

This raccoon intarsia combines all three. Start by numbering all the pieces on your master pattern.

Step 1: Choose your wood. Most of the raccoon's face is made from western red cedar. Aspen is used for the white parts. The slab is spalted walnut. The eyes are walnut dowels burnished with the Wonder Wheel (see sidebar). A small aspen dowel gives the eye its whiteness. We use aspen because it doesn't yellow when you apply a finish (see tip below).

Step 2: Make six copies of the pattern. Trim and sort according to the wood colors. Attach the pattern to your workpiece. Pay attention to grain direction and any "figures" in the wood such as knots or spalting. Try to work the figures into your intarsia.

Step 3: Cut out the pieces. Number the pieces, as you cut them out, to keep them straight.

Step 4: Cut out the ¼"-thick raising shims. Make sure the shims are undersized, so they don't interfere with the other pieces.

Step 5: Hand sand the back of the pieces. This will remove any burrs or tearout.

TIP | **ALTERNATIVE WHITE WOODS**

Other light woods, such as basswood or white pine, can be used for the white sections. These woods turn yellow after you add the polyurethane, so use one coat of a white polyurethane gel on them. The white gel is similar to the standard gel, but with white pigment added to keep the wood white.

6

Step 6: Attach the pieces to the sanding shim. Use double-sided carpet tape. Sanding shims are used to hold pieces in place while they are shaped on the pneumatic drum sander. This whole project is attached to a raising shim, so the raising shims can be used as sanding shims.

Texturing Intarsia with the Wonder Wheel

The Wonder Wheel, available through www.intarsia.com, is a great way to add texture to your intarsia. On soft woods, such as western red cedar, it works great to carve in the short, deep strokes that simulate the raccoon's bushy coat. On harder woods, such as the walnut we used for the raccoon's eyes, it actually burns the wood, giving you a dark, rich color.

The Wonder Wheel replaces the wheel in a grinder that runs between 3,450 and 4,000 rpm—be sure to follow the rotation arrows on the wheel. The wheel comes flat from the factory—so we use coarse sandpaper (40- to 60-grit) stapled to a piece of flat wood to give the wheel a V-shape.

The V does need to be re-sharpened from time to time. If you find that the wheel dances around or is hard to control, it may need sharpened. For rough coats, such as the raccoon's coat or a bear's coat, keep the wheel sharp and make short, deep cuts. For softer coats, such as a collie's coat or a horse's mane, let the wheel get a little dull (rounded) and make long, flowing strokes. Practice going with the grain and across the grain to produce different textures.

Inlay intarsia
in a spalted
slab for a
different look.

Step 7: Drill the ⅜"-diameter holes for the eyes. I use black walnut dowels for the eyes and add an aspen dowel to the center for contrast. Cut the dowels to size (depending on how deep the hole was drilled) and mark the location of the eye highlight with white typing correction fluid. Drill the ⅟₁₆"-diameter hole for the aspen dowel before rounding over the eye.

Step 8: Shape the pieces so they flow naturally from high to low. Use the pneumatic drum sander. Obviously, the raccoon's nose will be the highest point and the background will be the lowest.

Step 9: Sand down a piece of aspen until it will fit in a pencil sharpener. Sharpen the aspen into a cone shape using the pencil sharpener. Apply some wood glue to the aspen, and push it into the hole in the eye. Allow it to dry thoroughly, trim it off close to the eye, and sand it smooth.

Step 10: Carve the raccoon's fingers into shape, using the Wonder Wheel.

Step 11: Texture the raccoon's coat, using the Wonder Wheel.

Step 12: Apply your finish to the top and sides of each piece. Do not apply finish to the back side. Apply a polyurethane wiping gel liberally with a foam brush. After a minute, wipe off the excess with a paper towel. Then use a new paper towel to buff the finish with the grain.

Step 13: Glue the pieces in place on the shims. Use a combination of hot-melt glue and wood glue. Make sure your hot-melt glue gun gets up to at least 350°— otherwise the glue will harden before you have a chance to assemble the project properly. We use the hot glue sparingly on a few key parts to prevent it from shifting as you glue the rest of the parts down. In this project use the hot glue on the two outer parts. Then use wood glue on the rest of the pieces.

Step 14: Glue the shims in place in the background.

Materials & Tools

Materials:
- ¾" x 4½" x 9" dark-shaded wood of choice (I use western red cedar)
- ¾" x 6" x 5" medium dark-shaded wood of choice (I use western red cedar)
- ¾" x 8" x 24" medium-shaded wood of choice (I use spalted walnut)
- ¾" x 5" x 11" light-shaded wood of choice (I use western red cedar)
- ¾" x 5" x 7" white shaded wood of choice (I use aspen)

- 2 each ⅜"-diameter walnut dowels ¾"-long
- Repositionable spray adhesive.
- ¼" x 18" x 24" lauan plywood for the backing and sanding shims
- Wood glue

Tools:
- Scroll saw blades of choice
- Pneumatic drum sander or flexible-drum sander
- Wonder Wheel

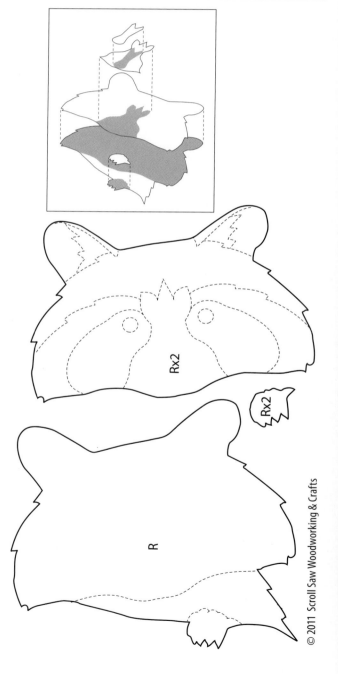

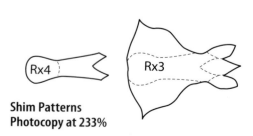

**Shim Patterns
Photocopy at 233%**

© 2011 Scroll Saw Woodworking & Crafts

Legend

→← Grain direction
D........Dark shade of wood
MD.....Medium dark shade of wood
M........Medium shade of wood
LT.......Light shade of wood
W.......White pine, aspen,
         or any white wood
R........These areas can be raised
         using ¼" plywood. (These
         areas can be raised
         in sections rather
         than individually.)

Rx2.....Raise these areas an
         additional ¼" making
         a total of ½" in shims.

Rx3.....Raise these areas an
         additional ¼" making
         a total of ¾" in shims.

Rx4.....Raise these areas an
         additional ¼" making
         a total of 1" in shims.

**Make at least 5 copies of
the Raccoon pattern.**

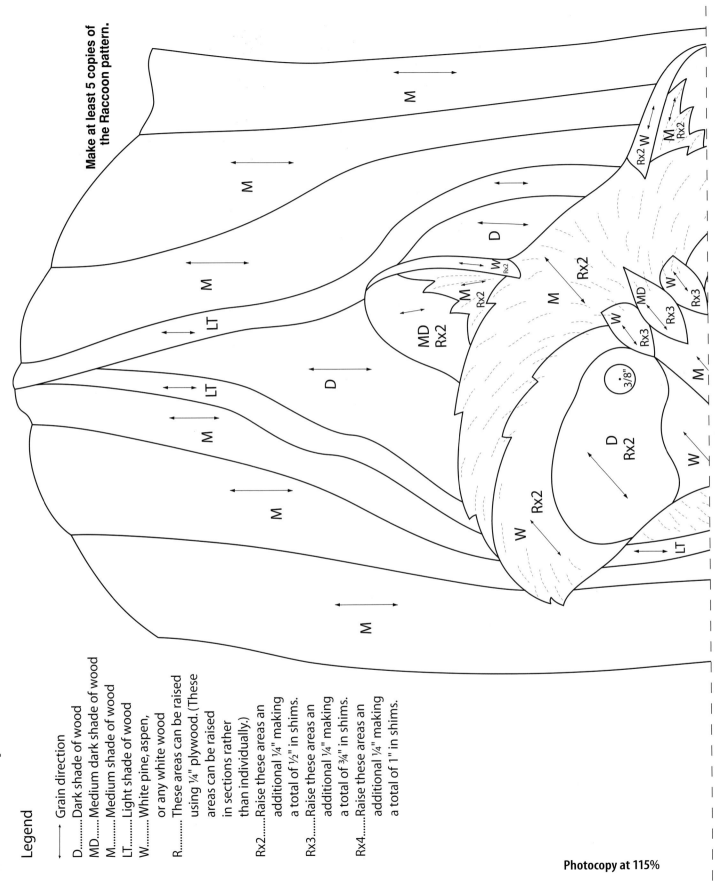

Photocopy at 115%

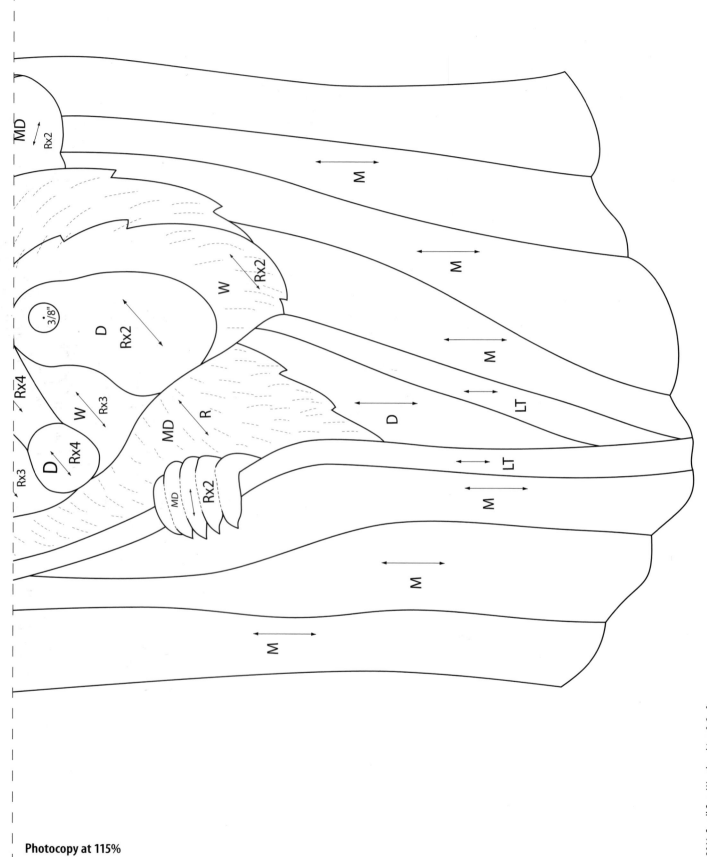

Photocopy at 115%

Think Pink

By Bob DeCuir

Scroll this flamingo wall plaque and add a little bit of tropical flair and color to your corner of the world. With its stark blue sky, pink flamingos and green leaves, this project simply jumps off the wall and will prompt many comments.

A fun project to make, it is the perfect gift for someone who's always seeking warmer climates. The key to success with this piece is to read your pattern completely so, on assembly, each leaf and flamingo is positioned and supported by dowel stock.

An elevated, see-through pattern makes it easier to assemble cut and painted segments.

Step 1: Place the 12" x 12" plastic sheet over the layout pattern. Use a marking pen to trace the pattern onto the surface of the plastic. Mount the four dowel legs to each corner using round-headed screws. (The legs are just stand-offs to hold the overview panel during assembly.) Cut them long enough so you have unrestricted movement under the surface as you guide your pieces into alignment with the layout pattern. Set the plastic assembly viewer aside until you're ready to assemble the plaque.

Step 2: Using temporary bond spray adhesive or rubber cement, adhere the five flamingo patterns to the wood. Then, using double-sided carpet tape, mount a piece of contrasting wood to the underside of the flamingo bill. Be sure to mount a temporary (same thickness) piece as an outrigger to stabilize your cut. (See the tip box on using an outrigger.) Drill a blade-entry hole next to your starting point and cut the bill section keeping the blade at a 90-degree angle. Set the pieces aside when cut, marking each piece as you go. (Example: 1-A. Flamingo 1, bill piece A.) Repeat this process for each of the remaining flamingos so that A, B, C, and D are now set aside.

Step 3: Using a small belt sander or a hand sander, slightly round over the edges of all pieces. I use a finish sander or sometimes a soft-pad hand sander with 220-grit garnet paper. Assemble the four bill pieces and glue the contacting edges to each other to form a bill.

Step 4: Finish cutting out the bodies of the five birds. Round over all edges except the bill connecting point. Now glue the bill to the body and set it aside to dry. Once dry, only touch-up sanding should be required. For touch-up sanding, I use a soft-pad hand sander with 220-grit garnet paper. Mount the eyes in the location shown using epoxy glue.

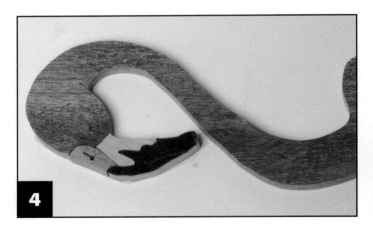

4

TIP | **USING RITE DYE**

Rite Dye is a fabric dye found in grocery stores that works well to dye wood. If you are using the dye with very hard wood, soak the pieces longer for a more vivid stain.

TIP | **WHAT'S AN OUTRIGGER?**

Generally speaking, an outrigger is a name for a temporary support. When you put a small piece of scrap wood below your pattern piece, put another piece of the same thickness at other points so the piece will stay stable as you cut it.

Step 5: Mount the leaf patterns to the poplar wood using rubber cement or spray glue. Cut all centerlines using a #2 reverse-tooth blade so they remain distinct. Dip the leaves in the green dye to color them a dark to light shade, as the leaves are naturally. To create the different shades from light to dark green, leave the wood in the dye for a shorter or longer time. When the leaves are dry, lightly hand sand 320-grit sandpaper to remove the fuzz with.

Step 6: Take the piece of wood for the background and trace the pattern shape onto its surface. Notice the dashed lines in the lower section under the leaves and flamingo mounting area. Be sure to mark these lines and cut them as illustrated. This area provides support for your stack process when you assemble.

Step 7: Cut out the background using a #5 reverse-tooth blade. Round over the sky edges before painting. Take note of the general view and paint the exposed sky area blue. Leave a bare wood spot to glue the sun in place.

8

To hang this piece, try using a keyhole router bit so the piece can lie flat against the wall. Hanging a project like this one can be difficult because of the weight distribution of the collective wood assembly. The multiple pieces in layers can shift your center away from the middle of the background piece. To find the center, take an awl with a sharp point and stick it into the back of the piece at about a 30-degree angle, pointing upward. In front of a small mirror, lift the piece and note which side is heavy. Reposition the awl until the piece hangs evenly; you have now found the center for that piece. Route the key or install the mount of your choice.

There are many ways to sign your work. I prefer to use a computer and an image transfer technique. Using a business card or label layout program, I print my shop name, centered on the first line; my name, centered on the second line; the place, month, and year, centered on the third line and an image of my signature, centered on the last line. When I print, I tell the program to send it to the printer in mirror image. I use a laser printer, but you could also use a copy machine, if desired. Because both laser printers and copy machines use heat-applied toner to print the image, you can then transfer the image to the wood using an iron set at "cotton," or a pattern transfer tool (a small soldering iron with a flat face tip the size of a quarter). Once the heat transfers the image to the wood, apply finish and your signature is locked and permanent.

Materials & Tools

Materials:
- ¼" pink ivory or a suitable substitute (flamingos)
- ¼" poplar (leaves)
- ¾" x 10" x 10" pine or wood of choice (sky and background)
- ⅛" x 4" x 4" lemon or pau amarillo (sun)
- ¼" elm and alder or contrasting scrap wood (A and B of bill)
- ¼" ebony or a suitable substitute (C and D, lower part of bill)
- Five ⁹⁄₃₂" craft store "eyes"
- ⅛"-diameter dowel (supports)
- Sandpaper, 220 and 320 grits
- Temporary bond spray adhesive or rubber cement
- Clear coat finish spray
- Sky blue paint (background sky)
- Lockwood's #4150 Moss Green water stain, Rite Dye, or wood coloring stain (leaves)

- Double-sided carpet tape
- Epoxy glue for the eyes
- Yellow wood glue
- ⅛" x 12" x 12" plastic sheet (assembly viewer, can be made thicker or from scrap on hand)
- 4, ½"-diameter dowels (legs of assembly view frame)
- 4 round-headed screws

Tools:
- #5, #2, and #2/0 reverse-tooth blades
- Drill with ¹⁄₁₆"-diameter bit
- Small belt sander or hand sander for surface of scrolled pieces
- Tweezers
- Marking pen
- 1" paintbrush (painting background)

Step 8: Place the background under the plastic assembly viewer. Using tweezers, assemble the flamingos and leaves in order using yellow glue and dowel supports. To begin assembly, study the overall layout until the stacking sequence makes sense. Spot-glue the base of each leaf or flamingo to the next in the stack. Support the flamingos with a small dowel glued to the underside and then glued to the background. The leaves are small enough that they don't need a dowel support. When the assembly is complete, set aside to dry completely. If you use a quick-setting variety of yellow wood glue, the assembly should take about an hour to dry.

Step 9: Use a small brush to touch up any bare or exposed spots.

Step 10: Spray a clear finish of your choice on the front and back. Be sure to sign and date your piece.

Blue Sky

Sun

Photocopy at 180%

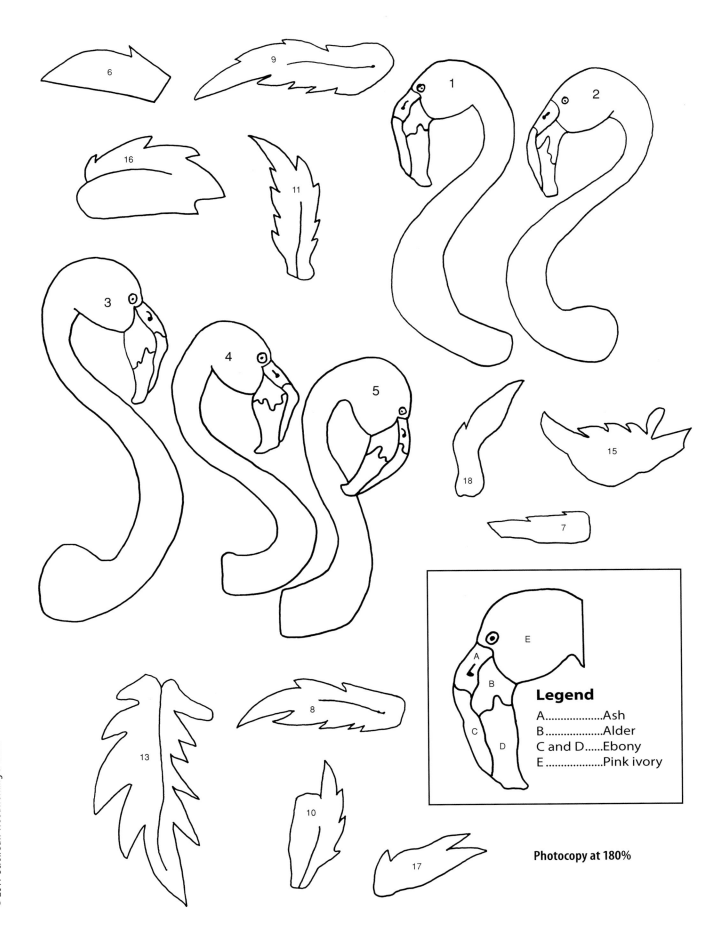

Legend

A..................Ash
B..................Alder
C and D......Ebony
E..................Pink ivory

Photocopy at 180%

Fox Portrait

By Neal Moore

The inspiration for the fox came to me while researching the raccoon. I wanted to capture his attitude and am pleased with the end result. The fox portrait was donated to the Roane-Jackson Technical Center along with a few other pieces. They were raffled off to help fund a trip for a group of student nurses to travel to California and take part in a national competition.

Staining Chart

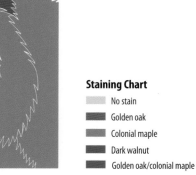

No stain

Golden oak

Colonial maple

Dark walnut

Golden oak/colonial maple

Photocopy at 100%

Spirited Colt Intarsia

By Kathy Wise

This adorable spring colt can be as easy or as challenging to create as you want. The paint version requires more precise cutting and fitting where the different colors of wood meet. For an easier project, make a bay, palomino, or solid color colt.

To get started, make several copies of the pattern. Always keep a master copy for later use. After you decide which colt to make, use a highlighter to mark the lines you want to cut. Cut the pattern pieces along the lines you marked, and separate them into piles based on the colors required.

It is important to start with flat wood for a good cut and fit. Plane any wood that is not flat. Make sure your blade is square to the saw table. Cut a piece of scrap wood, and check the cut edge with a small square. Adjust the table until the cut edge is square.

Apaloosa

Paint

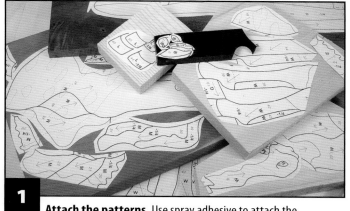

1

Attach the patterns. Use spray adhesive to attach the patterns to the shiny side of contact paper. Cut around the pattern pieces. Attach a full pattern to the backing board. Peel and stick the pattern pieces onto your selected wood. Line up the pattern pieces using the grain-direction arrows.

2

Cut the pieces. Some sections, where the color and grain direction are the same, can be cut at the same time. Cut the large section first with a #5 reverse-tooth blade. Cut the large section into smaller sections with a #2 or #3 blade. Number each piece on the bottom. Leave the base as one large piece for now.

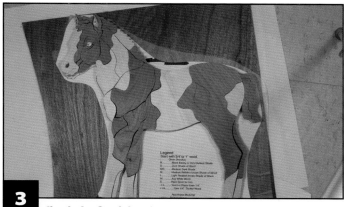

3

Check the fit of the pieces. Position the pieces on the pattern attached to the backing board. Make sure you like the grain pattern and color of the wood you selected for each piece in relation to the other pieces. If you don't like the fit, color, or grain, now is the time to make a change.

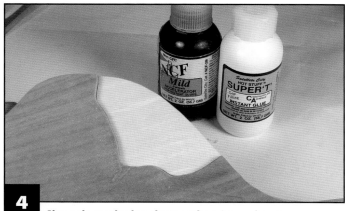

4

Glue select color breaks together. Areas where two colors join, but make up the same section, such as the legs or rump, should be shaped as one. Use cyanoacrylate (CA) glue to attach these areas together so you can shape them as one piece. If you are doing the single-color colt, this step is not necessary.

Customize this classic colt design to match your favorite color or breed of horse.

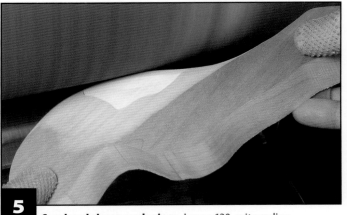

5 **Sand and shape each piece.** I use a 120-grit sanding drum on an 8" pneumatic-drum sander to start, then switch to 220-grit sandpaper on a 2" drum to smooth and shape the tight curves. Pencil in guide marks and check the fit with adjoining pieces often. Re-mark areas to shape and sand again as needed.

6 **Repair any gaps.** Mix CA glue with a bit of sawdust, and press the mixture into any small gaps. It acts as a custom color of wood putty. If the area joins two different colors, use sawdust from the darker color. If you have a large gap, the project will look better if you recut the pieces for a better fit.

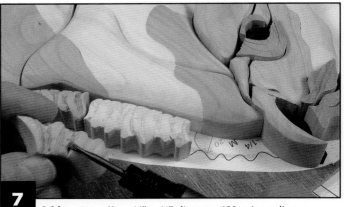

7 **Add texture.** Use a ½" or ¼"-diameter 120-grit sanding drum to shape small pieces that can't be reached with the drum sander. I use a cutting disc in an air grinder to cut grooves in the mane and tail. Add shims to the eye and nostril. Use a carving or hobby knife to clean up the areas around the mouth and nose.

8 **Finish sanding the pieces.** Use a fine-grit sanding mop to quickly remove any scratches. The mop gets into the curves and crevices and adds a beautiful sheen. It is possible to hand sand the pieces, but be sure to sand with the grain; any sanding done across the grain will show up when you apply the finish.

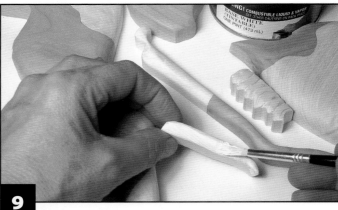

9 **Apply a white gel stain to the white wood areas.** Some finishes add a yellow cast to white wood. To prevent that, carefully apply white gel stain to the white areas. Use caution in areas where white wood is glued to a darker wood. Wipe the gel stain off with a rag or cotton swab.

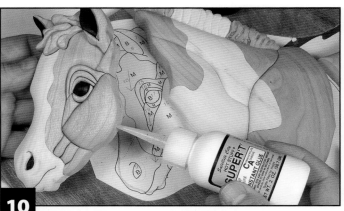

10 **Glue some sections together.** Make sure the sections fit tightly and are flat as you go along. Use CA glue to join individual sections. If you sand for fit, reapply the gel stain on any sanded white areas. Once the colt is assembled, trace the hooves onto the base piece. Then cut the base into sections for a good fit.

11 **Cut the backing board.** Position the assembled piece on the pattern for the backing board. Trace around the piece, making any necessary adjustments to the pattern. Cut ⅛" inside of your lines. Mark the glue side and sand the edges and both sides of the board. Stain or spray paint the edges and back of the board.

12 **Glue the piece to the backing board.** Spread wood glue evenly on the backing board. If the glue is too thick, it may squeeze up between pieces. Use a few drops of CA glue and accelerator to secure the piece until the wood glue dries. Clamp the piece to the backing board, and let the glue dry overnight.

13 **Apply the finish.** Gel varnish protects the wood and brings out the rich color. Wipe or brush the varnish onto the piece and wipe off the excess. Use an air compressor to blow the gel out of the cracks. Use cotton swabs to clean out other small areas. Apply two coats and allow them to dry overnight.

Materials & Tools

Materials:
- 1" x 10" x 24" medium wood such as cherry (body)
- 1" x 8" x 18" white wood such as poplar (body)
- ½" x 3" x 3" black wood such as ebony (eye & ears)
- 1" x 2" x 2" light wood such as ash (hooves)
- ½" x 4" x 18" dark wood such as black walnut (base)
- ¼" x 18" x 21" plywood or masonite (backing board)
- Roll of clear shelf contact paper
- Spray adhesive
- Wood glue
- Gel natural varnish or spray varnish
- White base gel varnish
- Wiping rags
- Hanger
- Cyanoacrylate glue and accelerator
- Cotton swabs
- 120-grit and 220-grit sanding sleeves

Tools:
- #2 or #3 & #5 reverse-tooth blades or blades of choice
- Pneumatic-drum sander
- Air grinder with ¼"- or ½"- diameter sanding drum
- Cutting disc for air grinder
- Hobby knife or carving knife
- Sanding mop
- Paintbrushes

14 **Complete the piece.** Add a dot of white paint to the eye for a highlight. Once the paint is dry, apply a clear gloss to the eye for a lifelike look. Attach your choice of hanger to the backing board to complete the project. Be sure to sign and date your work.

Breed Marking Guides

Palomino

Paint

Bay

Appaloosa

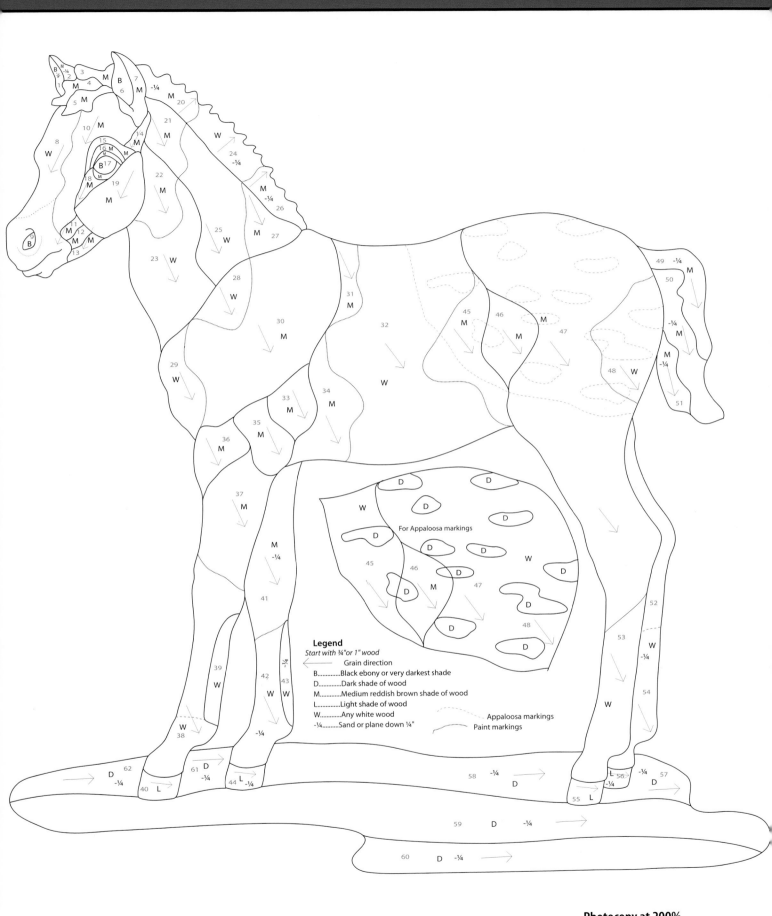

Legend

Start with ¾"or 1" wood

← Grain direction

B............Black ebony or very darkest shade
D............Dark shade of wood
M............Medium reddish brown shade of wood
L............Light shade of wood
W............Any white wood
-¼...........Sand or plane down ¼"

〜〜〜 Appaloosa markings
· · · · · Paint markings

For Appaloosa markings

Photocopy at 200%

Raccoon Portrait

By Neal Moore

This raccoon design was created for my granddaughter, Megan, who wanted "a ratcoon picture" for her bedroom. I use stain to color the different segments. The raised and lowered pieces add to the realism of the portrait.

Hot-melt glue is used to assemble the segments; it is strong enough to hold the portrait together, but easy enough to break loose if I decide I want to change the elevation of a piece.

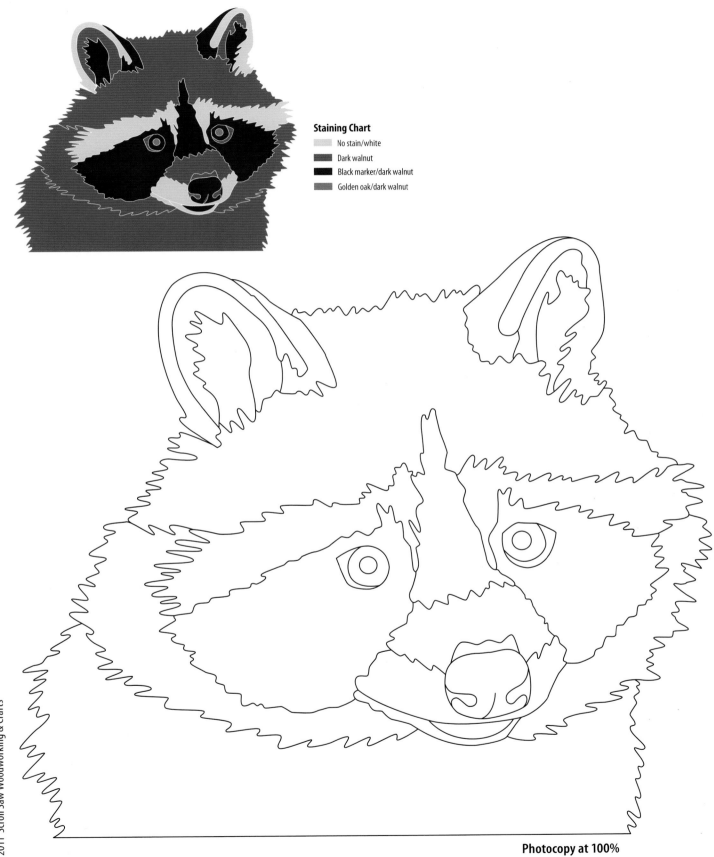

Staining Chart

No stain/white

Dark walnut

Black marker/dark walnut

Golden oak/dark walnut

Photocopy at 100%

Calico Cat Intarsia

By Kathy Wise

If you're looking for a purr-fect intarsia project, this calico or tortoiseshell cat makes a welcome addition to the art collection of any cat fancier. The different species of wood used will form the beautiful combination of black-, white-, and rust-colored fur. I used mahogany, black walnut, and basswood. The eyes and nose were cut out of locust wood. The black eye insert is ebony. You also can customize the pattern for other cat colors and markings, perhaps even to match your own pet.

Thanks to my father-in-law, Phil MacDonald, for his help cutting the project.

Side view shows layers on this calico cat intarsia piece.

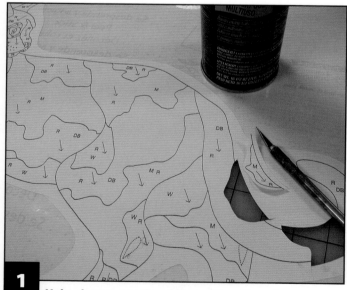

1 **Make about ten copies of the pattern.** Always keep a master copy to use later. Cut out and group pattern pieces together by color: dark, medium, light, and so on. Adhere color groups onto legal-size paper with glue stick. Copy each set of color-sorted patterns; save a copy for future use. Tape contact paper flat on a board. Spray adhesive on the pattern and contact paper and put together. Cut out each paper pattern piece.

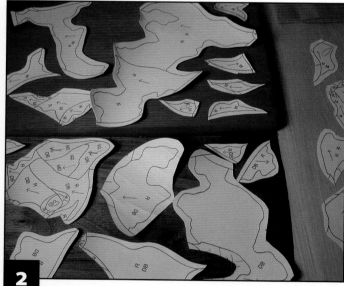

2 **Select your wood color.** It is very important to pick a good color and grain pattern for each separate intarsia piece. Your finished calico cat will be much more appealing with careful planning. Pick wood colors that will be close to a real calico cat's coloring. Peel and stick the pattern pieces on your selected pieces of wood. The contact paper will enable you to reposition your pattern piece if you change your mind on grain direction.

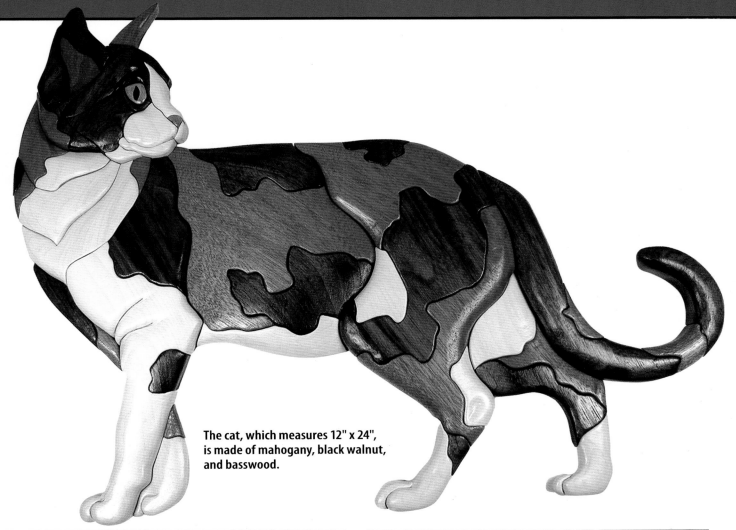

The cat, which measures 12" x 24", is made of mahogany, black walnut, and basswood.

3 **Check your blade angle.** Make sure your #5 blade is square to the saw table. Equally important is having flat wood for a good cut and fit. Plane any wood that is not perfectly flat. Using a scroll saw, cut out all the pieces using ¾"-thick wood.

4 **Cut out your backer board using ¼" plywood.** Use a full pattern and cut inside of the outside lines about ¹⁄₁₆" all the way around. Sand and stain just the edges. Mark your glue side. For this project it's pretty clear which side is the front, but some projects are more symmetrical and you can easily make a mistake and glue to the wrong side.

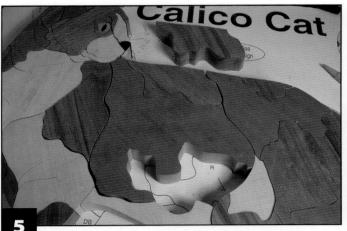

5 **Lay out all the cut pieces as you get them done on a full pattern taped to a work board.** Check for fit and make adjustments as needed. Now is the time to make any wood color or grain direction changes if you do not like the overall look. On this project, I decided I did not like the direction of the grain pattern on two pieces. I recut and replaced both. Keep in mind that the entire piece will darken with the finish. It is a good idea to test the color of your wood before you start to cut. Take a small sample of the wood you plan on using and put some gel varnish on it to see what your final color will be.

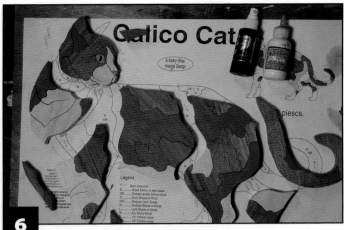

6 **To make shaping easier, group body sections together and glue with cyanoacrylate (CA) glue, using an accelerator to set up in ten seconds.** This glue technique is only temporary for sanding and shaping large sections and will break apart to sand the inside edges of each piece. See the tip box on the next page.

7 **You can make your intarsia project come alive by carefully shaping your pieces to achieve varying depths.** I did most of the shaping and sanding using a pneumatic drum sander. I used an air tool with a ½" sanding band to get the small details and round inside edges that I couldn't reach with the big drum sander. As you work with the pieces, try to visualize the different levels of a real cat's body. If you have a cat in the family, take a look over its face, legs, and ears. The careful shaping of the varying levels will give a nice 3-D feel to the finished piece. Don't be afraid to experiment. You can always recut another piece.

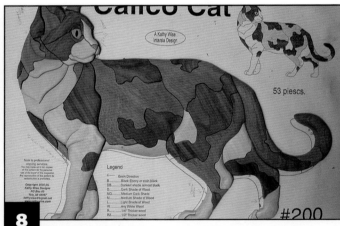

8 **Lay out the shaped pieces on a full pattern.** Make any final sanding adjustments. Lay out on backer board to check fit. Any trimming of overhanging edges can be done with a sanding tool after the pieces are glued to the backer board. Then simply retouch up the bare edges with dark stain.

9 **Apply varnish finish.** Using a soft rag, hand wipe Bartley's White Base gel stain on the white pieces. Let set a few minutes and wipe off with another clean rag. Let dry overnight. Put a coat of gel varnish on all white pieces and let dry overnight. Apply final coat of varnish. Using a soft rag, hand wipe natural gel varnish on all other pieces. Wipe off with a clean rag. Let dry, then put on a second coat.

10 **Glue together and finish.** I like to tack together sections of my project with 100% silicone glue. This prevents them from sliding and moving when I glue. Group together the head, leg, body, and tail sections. Place a small drop or two of glue between your pieces, press together, and arrange on a pattern board for correct placement. Let dry overnight.

Materials:

- ¾" x 12" x 12" dark walnut (D)
- ¾" x 8" x 10" white basswood (W)
- ¾" x 8" x 10" mahogany (M)
- ¾" x 2" x 2" locust (Y)
- ¾" x 3" x 3" light oak or other light wood (L)
- ¾" x 2" x 2" ebony (B)
- ¼" x 24" x 12" plywood for backer
- Roll of clear shelf contact paper
- Temporary bond spray adhesive
- Yellow wood glue
- Cyanoacrylate glue

Materials & Tools

- Quick-set accelerator
- Gel natural varnish and base white gel stain
- Wiping rags
- Sawtooth hanger
- 100% silicone caulk

Tools:

- #5 blade
- Drill with ³⁄₁₆"-diameter bit
- Pneumatic-drum sander
- Rotary carving tool with sanding band
- ½" sanding drum

11 **Arrange and glue pieces to backer board using yellow wood glue.** If you need to realign a silicone-tacked piece, simply pull apart. Glue and weigh down with sand bags or clamp. Let dry overnight and then put on one more finish coat of varnish on your cat. Saturate a cloth, squeeze out the excess and wipe a light coat of varnish on the entire project. Attach a sawtooth hanger and your calico cat project is finished.

Use CA Glue to Hold Sections Together for Sanding

Use cyanoacrylate glue with a quick-set accelerator to hold small or large sections together for shaping. Holding two pieces together, put one or two tiny drops of glue on the bottom. Add a quick spray of the accelerator to the bottom area. Set on a piece of scrap paper and make sure the pieces are completely flat and fit tightly. Do this quickly; it will set up in about ten seconds. Add other pieces one at a time, making sure they are flat. Too much glue will run onto the paper and make it difficult to break the pieces apart.

Now you can shape an entire leg or body section on the sanding drum and get a nice, even shape from one piece to the next. After shaping and sanding, sharply rap the section on a tabletop. It will come apart easily. Be careful with small delicate parts; too much force will break the wood apart. If two pieces don't separate, simply recut with the scroll saw on the parting line. Be patient; this technique takes a little practice, but the finished results make it well worth the effort.

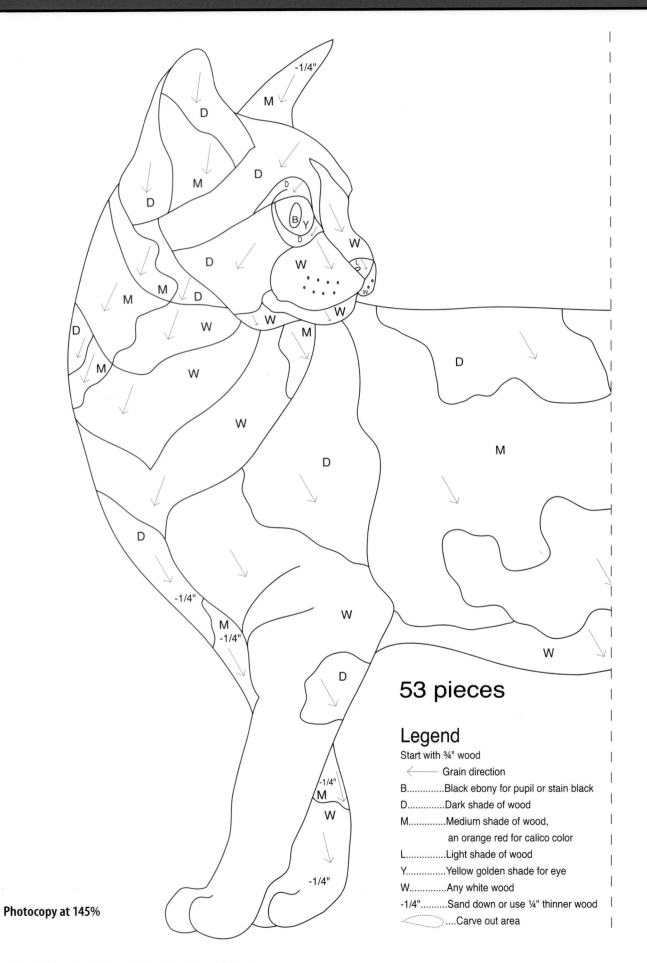

53 pieces

Legend

Start with ¾" wood

⟵   Grain direction

B..............Black ebony for pupil or stain black

D..............Dark shade of wood

M..............Medium shade of wood,
             an orange red for calico color

L..............Light shade of wood

Y..............Yellow golden shade for eye

W..............Any white wood

-1/4".........Sand down or use ¼" thinner wood

⬭ ....Carve out area

Photocopy at 145%

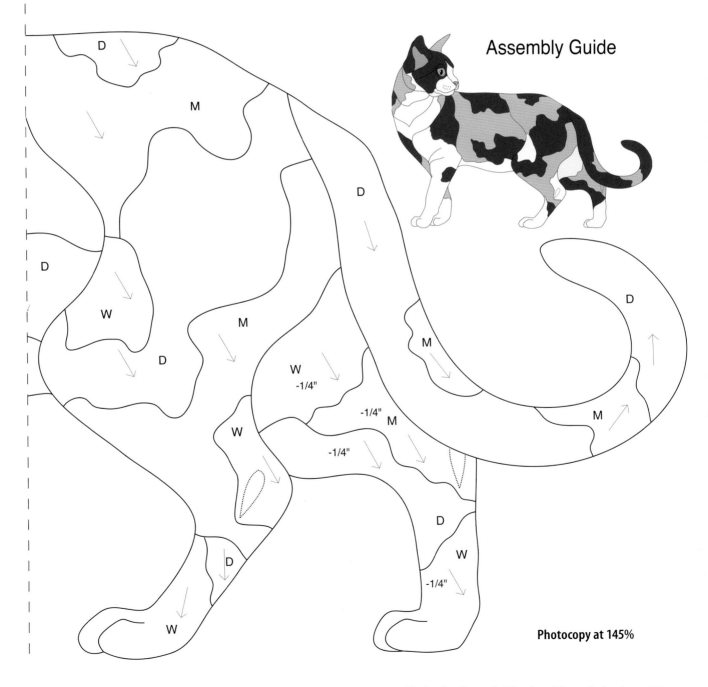

D

M

D

D

W

D

M

D

W

-1/4"

-1/4" M

-1/4"

W

W

D

D

W

-1/4"

M

M

D

M

Assembly Guide

Photocopy at 145%

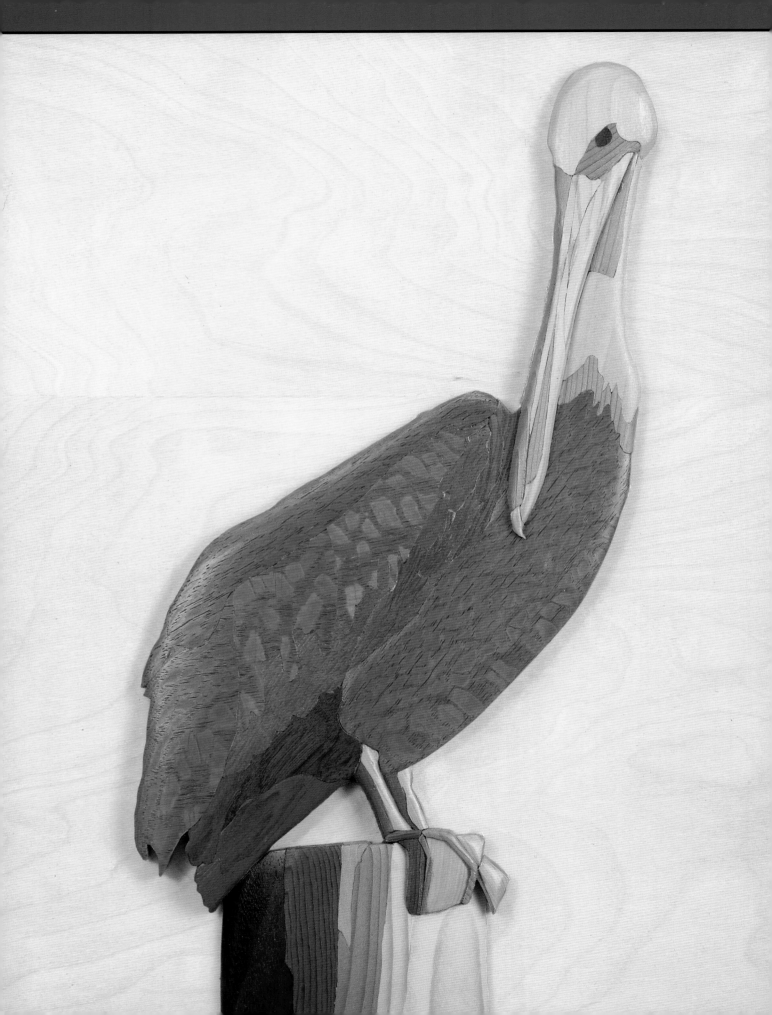

Brown Pelican Intarsia

By James R. West

A rustic frame of weathered wood accents the pelican portrait.

I have made many projects from commercial patterns and finally decided it was time to create my own. Finding the right image is important. The brown pelican began when I saw a picture a friend had—it was an image I felt compelled to make. Make sure the image you are using is copyright-free or you have the photographer's permission to use it when making the pattern.

Making the Pattern
Start by scanning the image into a computer. While not necessary, it is helpful because you can print the image at any size. I print both color and black and white copies. If you want a larger size, print the image in overlapping sections and splice them together. Using a light table or backlit piece of frosted glass makes this task much easier.

I use the color copy as a reference and the black and white copy to trace the pattern. This makes it easier to determine where to make the wood color and grain-direction changes. You have to find a happy medium between detail and practicality. If the pieces are too small, the detail is overwhelming. If they're too big, fit and warping can become a problem.

Wood Selection
Wood selection is critical. Color, grain pattern, and structure all affect the final appearance. Visualize the finished project in your mind, and make notes on the pattern to reflect your mental image. I had a piece of lacewood that was wonderfully figured and took advantage of this effect to accent the flow of the feathers on the body.

I've found that using different thicknesses of stock can add quite a bit of depth to the project. I resaw woods on the band saw to a variety of thicknesses, usually in ⅛"-increments. It saves time sanding and thinner stock is much easier to cut. I use ½"-thick as the base thickness on all my projects.

On this project, the head and bill were cut from ⅝"-thick stock, and the leg, which is farther away in the picture, was cut from ⅜"-thick stock. Once the finished project was shaped and the varying heights were blended, the 3-D effect was achieved.

Applying the Pattern
I make all of the copies needed for the project at the same time and overlap areas that are too big to fit on one page. There is some distortion inherent in photocopies, but making all of the copies at the same time minimizes that.

To glue the pattern pieces down, I use spray adhesive, but on the small pieces, some of the craft-rated sprays do not hold well. Experiment with the different types of adhesives and determine how heavy to spray it onto the pattern to find what works best for you.

Finishing
Finish on the project is a personal preference. For its long-lasting qualities and low maintenance, I use an oil-based varnish. Many patterns recommend a custom-cut backing board for a stand-alone appearance, but I usually add a frame to all of my pieces. For this project, I used a Baltic birch backer and made a rustic frame from weathered oak that spent the first 50 years of its existence as the handles on a wheelbarrow. Don't be tempted to cut corners in this area. A distinct frame can really enhance the appeal of your project.

Materials & Tools

Materials:
- ¾" x 1½" x 5" poplar
- ¾" x 4" x 4" light cedar
- ¾" x 4" x 7" medium cedar
- ½" x 7" x 10" dark cedar (lacewood)
- ½" x 1½" x 3" black walnut
- ¾" x ¾" x 4½" yellow pine
- ⅜" x 4¾" x 2" white pine
- 14⅞" x 22¼" Baltic birch backer board
- Oil-based varnish of choice
- Assorted grits of sandpaper

Tools:
- Scroll saw blades of choice
- Sanding tools of choice (I use a random-orbit palm sander and a belt sander)
- Band saw (optional for re-sawing wood)

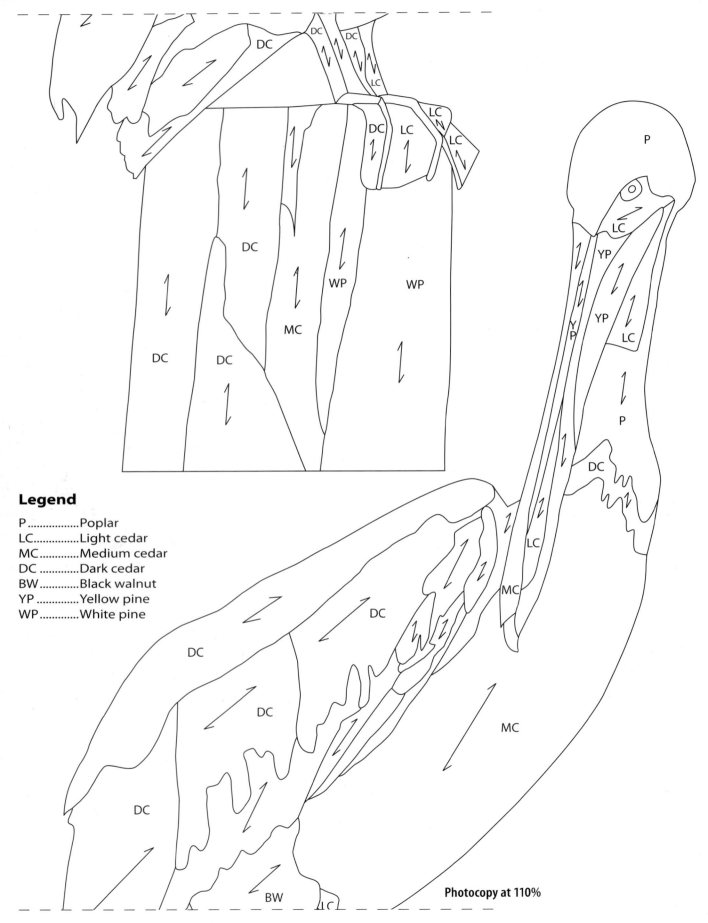

Legend

P ....Poplar
LC ....Light cedar
MC ....Medium cedar
DC ....Dark cedar
BW ....Black walnut
YP ....Yellow pine
WP ....White pine

Photocopy at 110%

Bobcat on the Rocks

By Janette Square

An exceptional intarsia piece relies on pattern design, wood selection, and cutting and shaping skills. The same design completed by different artists can produce dramatically different results.

Time spent choosing the right wood for each section will be evident in the finished project. Consider the color, grain, and thickness of your potential selections. Plan the placement of each pattern piece, taking advantage of the figure of the wood to enhance the project. Trace the pattern onto clear plastic. Hold the clear pattern on the wood and slide it around until you find the perfect grain for the piece. Place cut pieces on top of the clear pattern to aid in your selection.

I use myrtle for the bobcat. Myrtle is a hard wood and burns easily when you are cutting and shaping.

Use clear packaging tape to help lubricate the blade and make pattern removal easy. When working with hard woods, it is easy to start pushing the wood through the blade to go faster, especially as the blade

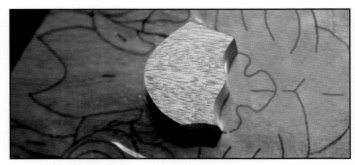

A transparent pattern helps with wood selection.

dulls. Let the blade do the cutting. Excessive force can result in bowed edges. I frequently check the edges of cut pieces to make sure they are square. If you do find bowed edges, use a spindle sander to square the piece before moving on to the next section. Change the blade frequently. If you find the wood starting to burn as you're cutting, try cutting from the other direction. The grain direction can affect the amount of burning.

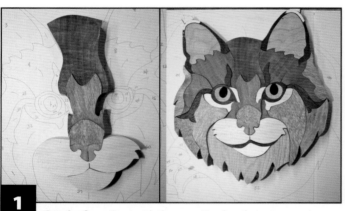

1 **Cut the face.** Start with the nose. Number the pattern and the bottom of each piece as you cut it. Assemble the pieces on a master pattern to check for fit and wood selection. Leave the small tufts on the tips of the ears connected to the ears for now.

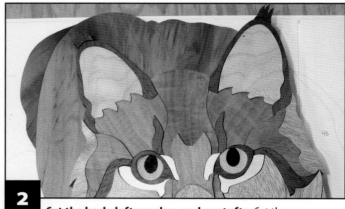

2 **Cut the back, left rear leg, and ear tufts.** Cut the outline of the back pieces. Cut the area for the ear tuft in the back and then cut the ear tufts from the ears. Trace the outline of the back onto the stock for the left rear leg.

3 **Cut the right side and right rear leg.** The grain direction runs the same way for these two pieces, so you can cut both of them together and then cut the individual pieces apart.

4 **Cut the front legs and feet.** Do not cut the stripes that are totally surrounded by the leg. Cut the full stripes and the legs, including the feet. Make sure to align the grain direction of the stripes with the legs.

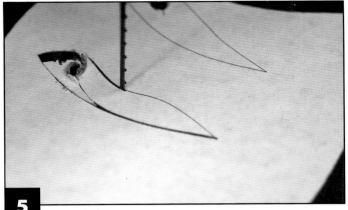

5 **Cut the inlay stripes.** Drill blade-entry holes in the leg for the inlay stripes. Follow the lines exactly and make sure the blade is square with the table. Follow the lines on the inlay stock and make sure these cuts are square as well.

6 **Cut the rocks and tree.** Make sure all of the pieces fit together tightly. Try to find interesting pieces that complement the cat, both in grain and coloring. You can carve in texture if you can't get the right effect with the wood's grain.

7 **Vary the thickness of the pieces.** You can use different thicknesses of wood, resaw the wood, or add shims under the wood. See the chart on the pattern for the recommended thicknesses of the different sections.

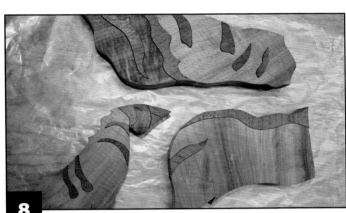

8 **Begin shaping the pieces.** Glue the leg pieces together; they will be shaped as units. Rough shape the pieces with a flexible-drum sander equipped with a 120-grit sanding drum. Switch to a 220-grit sanding drum to remove the scratches.

9 **Continue shaping the project.** Shape the rest of the project, leaving the face for last. The cat's front legs are resting on the rocks and should remain higher than the rocks for proper perspective. Polish the pieces with a 220-grit mop sander. Replace the pieces on the master pattern to check for fit and flow.

10 **Shape the face.** This is the trickiest part. Place the pieces in position away from the main project. Use a sanding drum in a rotary power carver to rough contour the pieces while they are in position. Smooth the pieces with the flexible-drum sander and then polish them with the mop sander. Glue the intarsia together.

11 **Apply the finish.** Apply a dot of antique white paint to each eye for a highlight. Position the project on a lazy susan. Apply gel varnish to the sides and top with a foam brush. Wipe off the excess with paper towels. Blow the excess out of the cracks with an air compressor or use a soft dental tool to remove it. Allow the varnish to dry overnight and apply a second coat.

12 **Assemble the project.** Trace the project onto a piece of ⅛"-thick Baltic birch plywood. Cut ⅛" inside the lines. Sand and bevel the edges of the backing board, darken the edges with a marker or black paint, and glue and clamp the intarsia to the backing board.

DESIGNED & MADE BY:
JANETTE SQUARE
PIECE # 19.05.07

WOODS USED:
BOBCAT - OREGON MYRTLEWOOD
PERUVIAN WALNUT
ASPEN
FIGURED MAPLE
CHERRY
SATINWOOD
EBONY
ROCKS - BUCKEYE BURL
BLUE PINE
Tree STUMP - SPALTED PIN OAK
WALNUT

13 **Sign and date your piece.** Attach a hanger to the back. Sign and date the back of the project. I use a permanent marker and include a list of all the woods used in the project.

Materials & Tools

Materials:
- 1" x 7" x 24" dark, striped myrtle (front legs and upper part of head)
- ⅝" x 12" x 12" darker-grained myrtle (back and rear legs)
- 1" x 8" x 8" light myrtle (lower face)
- 1" x 6" x 12" Peruvian walnut or dark wood of choice (stripes on legs, face, and mouth; outline of ears and eyes)
- 1" x 3" x 6" aspen or light wood of choice (muzzle, chin, around eyes)
- ¾" to 1" x 3" x 6" figured maple (insides of ears)
- 1" x 1" x 2" cherry (nose)
- 1" x 1" x 2" satinwood or yellowheart (eyes)
- ½" x ½" x 2" ebony (pupils, use a riser to conserve expensive ebony)
- ¾" x 5" x 16" buckeye burl (rocks)
- ¾" x 7" x 8" blue pine (rocks)
- ¾" x 4" x 7" spalted pin oak (tree stump)
- ¾"-thick scrap of walnut (center part of tree stump)
- Clear plastic (to trace pattern)
- Fine point permanent marker
- ⅛" x 24" x 24" Baltic birch plywood (backing board)
- Clear packaging tape
- Spray adhesive
- Sandpaper, 220 grit
- Assorted grits of sanding drum covers
- Wood glue
- Antique white acrylic paint (eye highlight)
- Black acrylic paint or large black marker (sides of backing board)
- Gel varnish
- Paper towels
- Hanger of choice
- Disposable foam brush

Tools:
- #7 reverse-tooth scroll saw blades or blades of choice (you'll use a lot)
- Flexible-drum sander
- Spindle sander
- Rotary power carver
- Sanding mops
- Air compressor (to remove finish from cracks)
- Rubber-tip dental tool (to remove excess finish)

Photocopy at 180%

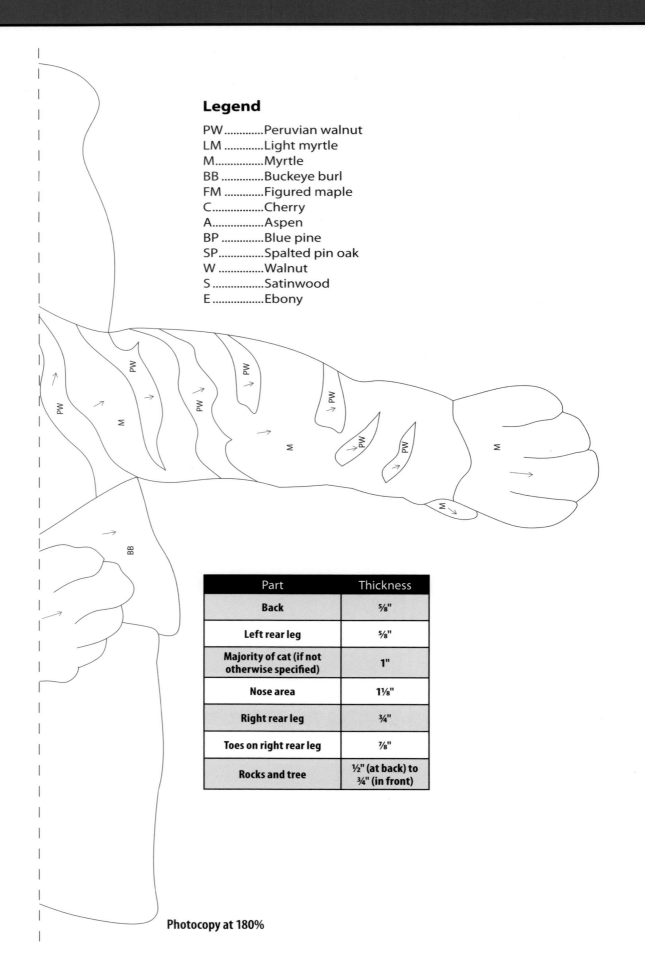

Legend

PW ....Peruvian walnut
LM ....Light myrtle
M................Myrtle
BB ....Buckeye burl
FM ....Figured maple
C................Cherry
A................Aspen
BP ....Blue pine
SP...............Spalted pin oak
W ....Walnut
S ....Satinwood
E ....Ebony

Part	Thickness
Back	⅝"
Left rear leg	⅝"
Majority of cat (if not otherwise specified)	1"
Nose area	1⅛"
Right rear leg	¾"
Toes on right rear leg	⅞"
Rocks and tree	½" (at back) to ¾" (in front)

Photocopy at 180%

Painted Pony

By James Haumesser

Always fascinated by carousel horses, I made several scaled-down versions of the famous painted ponies from commercially available intarsia patterns but felt something was missing. Then, while searching online, I found a Dentzel Carousel coloring book and started making my own simple patterns. They have become increasingly detailed over time.

Most carousel horses feature bright, vibrant colors, so I use paint to bring my pieces to life. I prefer to use 1⅛"-thick pine shelving material. Made of 1½"-wide strips, it generally does not warp like solid stock. I select the pieces with the fewest knots and then let them age for about a year.

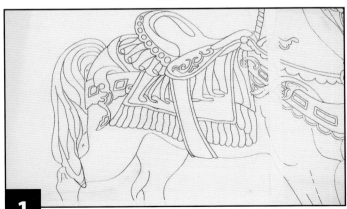

1

Transfer the pattern. Use a fine stylus and carbon or graphite paper to trace the pattern onto the wood. The finer the line, the more accurate the cuts will be. The head and the body usually fit onto two 18" blanks, with the tail and legs fitting onto the wood left over from the main sections.

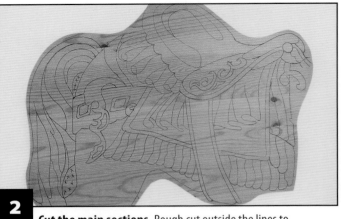

2 **Cut the main sections.** Rough cut outside the lines to separate the blank into sections. Make sure your blade is square to the table. Then cut along the lines and check the fit of the main sections. Accurate cutting and proper fitting will save you time during final assembly.

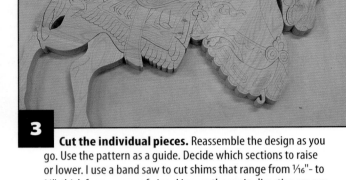

3 **Cut the individual pieces.** Reassemble the design as you go. Use the pattern as a guide. Decide which sections to raise or lower. I use a band saw to cut shims that range from 1/16"- to 1/4"-thick from scraps of pine. Line up the grain direction on any exposed shims with the adjoining project.

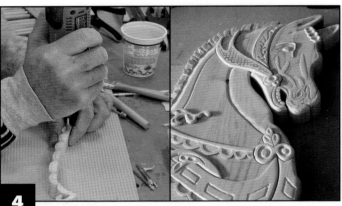

4 **Shape the pieces.** Use a variety of carving and shaping tools to add details to the mane, tail, harness, teeth, and any other areas desired. Use a router with a 1/4"-radius roundover bit to bevel any adjoining pieces that are not shaped. This bevel emphasizes segments that highlight the design.

5 **Sand and seal the pieces.** Sand all of the exposed wood with 180-grit sandpaper. Remove any sanding dust with compressed air. Apply a coat of an equal mix of shellac and denatured alcohol. This sealing coat minimizes raised grain after you apply the white acrylic paint primer.

6 **Apply the primer.** White is traditionally used as the primer for carousel horses. I use an airbrush to apply the paint and a liner brush for the fine details, but you can use a brush for everything. It generally takes at least two coats to obtain a consistent color.

7 **Apply the base coat.** Add one to two coats of the main solid color on the appropriate areas. You can follow my color scheme or create your own. Don't worry about the shading or details at this point; they will be added after the base coat dries.

8 **Add the shading.** Set the airbrush to a thin spray and hold it at a low angle to the surface. Imagine what areas would be shaded if light shown down on a pony. Add shadows and definition to those areas.

9 **Paint the detail areas.** I use fine brushes and thin the paint with water. Be sure to finish the sides and bottom edges of each piece. Because I mount the finished horse on a mirror, the bottom edge of the pieces can be seen in the reflection.

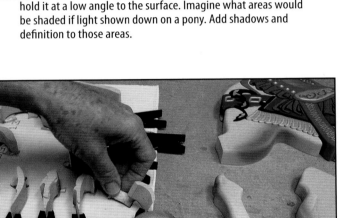

10 **Apply the clear finish.** Allow the paint to dry thoroughly. While acrylic paint dries quickly, it's best to allow the pieces to dry overnight. Then apply two coats of clear gloss acrylic varnish according to the manufacturer's instructions.

11 **Mount the project.** I attach the pieces to a mirror using silicone caulking, then use a razor and window-washing fluid to remove any caulk that squeezes out. You could trace around the pieces on a piece of plywood, then cut inside the lines for a traditional backing board. Attach the pieces with glue and use a weight to hold them in place until the glue dries.

TIP **PAINTING COLORS AND SET UP**

I avoid mixing special colors. It is often necessary to do touch-ups later, and it is difficult to make a good match unless you still have some of the custom color available.

Set up several cardboard sheets and arrange the pieces on individual sheets by color. Support the project pieces on small scraps to keep them from sticking to the cardboard. Apply the paint, then move onto the next sheet of cardboard and a new color.

Materials:
- 1⅛" x 18" x 4' pine shelf board or wood of choice
- Carbon paper or graphite paper
- Assorted grits of sandpaper up to 180-grit
- Shellac
- Denatured alcohol
- White acrylic paint (primer)
- Acrylic paint colors of choice
- Clear gloss acrylic varnish
- Wood glue or silicone caulk
- Framed mirror or plywood (backing board)
- Window washing fluid (for clean mirror)

Materials & Tools

Tools:
- #5 reverse-tooth blades or blades of choice
- Assorted carving and shaping tools of choice
- Router with ¼"-radius roundover bit
- Airbrush or assorted paintbrushes of choice
- Razor (to clean mirror)

These three pieces are cut from a separate piece of ⁵⁄₁₆" pine and glued in place.

Photocopy at 200%

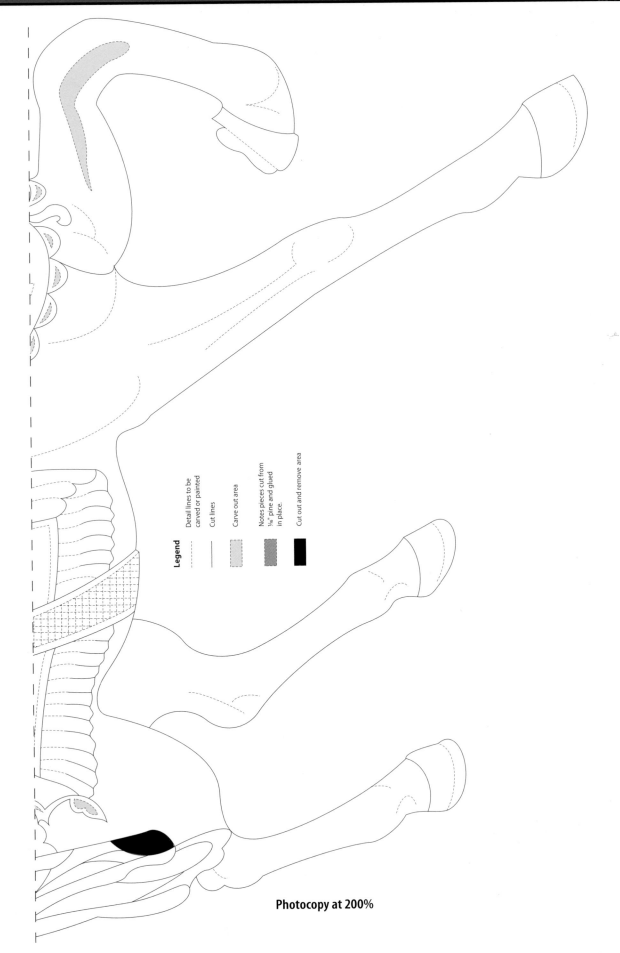

Legend

- - - - - Detail lines to be carved or painted
———— Cut lines
▨ Carve out area
▧ Notes pieces cut from 1/16" pine and glued in place.
█ Cut out and remove area

Photocopy at 200%

Majestic Elephant Mosaic

By Susan Mathis

The lines and wrinkles in an elephant's face are well suited for a mosaic treatment. The trick was capturing the creature's proud majestic look.

I cut the trunk into several pieces and stagger the sections for additional dimension. I support the trunk pieces with dowels and biscuits. For a simpler project, you can leave the trunk solid.

Number the pieces as you cut them. Sand and shape the individual pieces as desired. I add ⅛"-thick shims under the right ear, face, and trunk to add more depth.

Using the photo as a reference, color the pieces with thinned acrylic paint. I use light gray, medium gray, and dark gray for the head, white for the tusks, and black for the eyes. Add a dot of undiluted white to the eyes to make them sparkle.

Glue the project together and glue it to a backing board. I create the backing board for the trunk in sections and follow the contour of the trunk. Spray the project with one coat of sealer and let it dry completely.

To bring the portrait to life, I apply a wash of stain before the final coat of sealer. Practice this technique on a piece of scrap wood first. Working quickly, one section at a time, apply black stain with a brush or a rag. Wipe a little stain off with a clean rag. The amount you remove is up to you. Use the same technique on the rest of the project. Let the stain dry completely and apply a coat of spray sealer.

Materials & Tools

Materials:
- ¾" x 20" x 22" pine or wood of choice
- Assorted ⅛"-thick pieces of scrap (shims)
- ¼" x 20" x 22" hardboard or plywood (backing board)
- Spray adhesive
- Acrylic paint: white, black, light gray, medium gray, and dark gray
- Soft cloth
- Assorted paintbrushes
- Wood glue
- Sandpaper
- Black stain
- Flat spray lacquer or sealer of choice
- Dowels or joint biscuits (optional to reinforce trunk)

Tools:
- #5 reverse-tooth blades or blades of choice
- Hand rotary tool (optional for shaping)
- Drill with bit to fit dowels or router with biscuit-joint bit (optional)

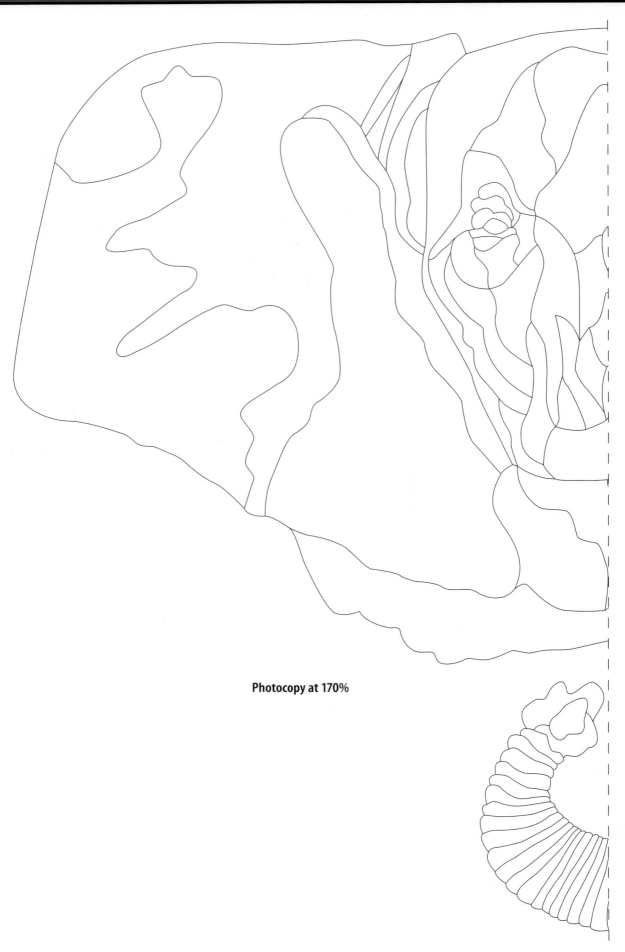

Photocopy at 170%

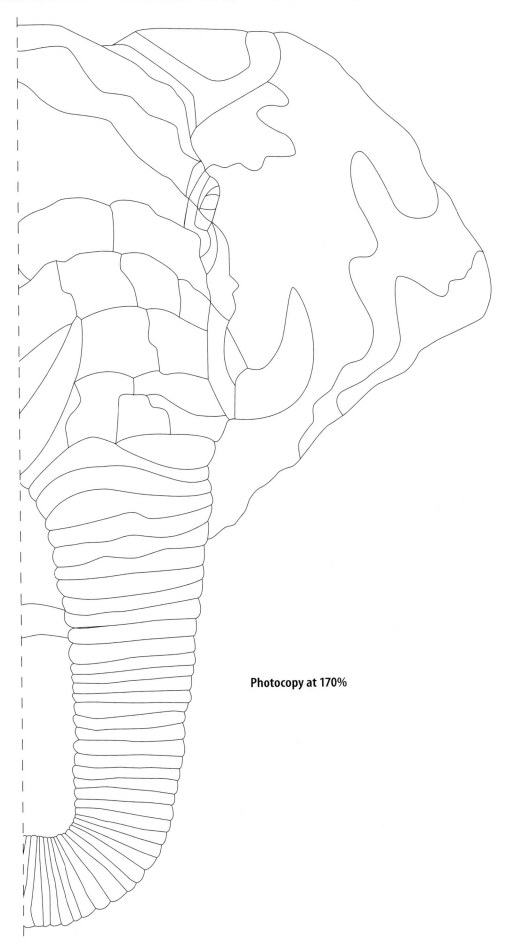

Photocopy at 170%

Spring Songbirds

By Janette Square
Design by Bruce Worthington

Intricate details really bring this piece to life. Bruce has taken great pains to make every aspect of the piece interesting. I love the slightly askew shingles on the birdfeeder roof and the bright colors brought in by representing several types of songbirds. As soon as Bruce shared the design with me, I knew I had to make it. This is a challenging project, but the end results are well worth the effort.

I approached this project differently than I usually do. Because of some of the smaller pieces, I found it easier to glue some pieces together as I went along. I broke the project down into more manageable segments to make it less intimidating. By cutting and shaping specific segments or elements before moving on to the next, I could see my progress, which kept me motivated.

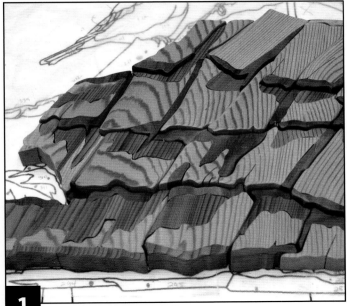

1 **Construct the roof.** Each shingle is made up of several pieces to create a weathered look. Color code and number the pattern, and select the woods you will use for each color. Cut and glue each shingle together. After the individual shingles are glued together, sand and shape each shingle. The top of the shingle is ⅛" lower than the bottom of the shingle, simulating a real roof. Once all of the shingles are shaped, glue the roof section together.

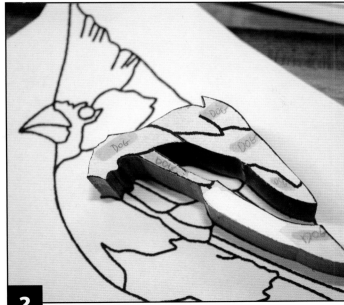

2 **Cut and shape each bird separately.** This way they can be fit into the birdfeeder individually. Most of the feathers can be cut as one piece; then the individual feathers can be cut. Shape each feather and glue it to the previous one as you go along. Shape and glue all the individual birds together. Paint a small dowel black or use a permanent marker for the eyes. Add a dot of white acrylic paint to the eyes for a highlight.

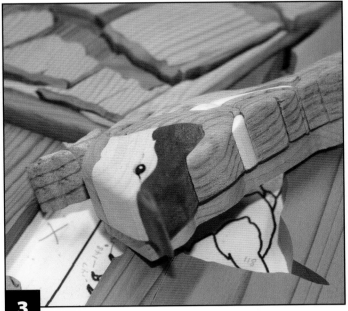

3 **Cut the rest of the birdfeeder.** When cutting the feeder, I cut straight across as if the bird wasn't there. Dry assemble the right side, place the nuthatch in position, and trace around it. Cut along the traced lines for a better fit. Add a ¼"-thick riser to the back of the nuthatch. Make sure the riser doesn't show when assembled. Cut the tray piece next. I glue the chickadee on top of the birdfeeder pieces, like an overlay, for more depth and dimension. I use the trace and cut method, as I did with the nuthatch, for the feet of the other three birds.

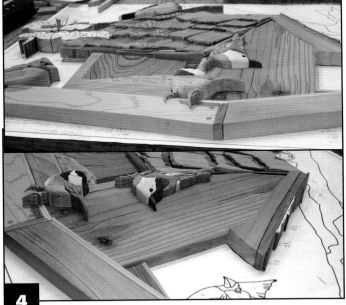

4 **Shape the pieces of the birdfeeder.** Reduce the thickness of the pieces for the main structure by ⅛". The tray portion is thicker. Taper the pieces that make up the back sides of the tray so they "disappear" behind the feeder. The left tray piece begins lower on the right, tapers up to meet the cardinal, and is level with the front piece. Taper the front part of the tray lower on the left; the right tray piece tapers slightly towards the right. Cut out and glue a ¼"-thick shim to the back of the shingled roof. The shim should not be visible after everything is glued together.

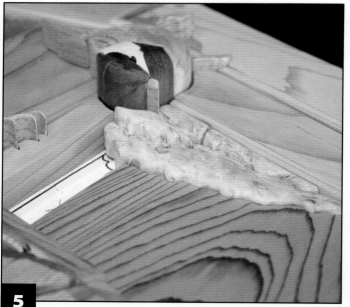

5 **Shape the birdseed and assemble the feeder.** The three birdseed sections should be raised by 1/16", 1/8", and 1/4" respectively to give the effect of depth and dimension. Burled wood gives a wonderful seed effect. If you don't have wood that resembles birdseed, you could texture those sections by dimpling the wood surface. Once you're satisfied with the shaping of the birdseed, lightly ease the edges with 220-grit sandpaper. Glue the birdseed, birdfeeder, nuthatch, and chickadee in place.

6 **Cut the leaves, small branch, and hanger.** The negative space in this project makes it easy to make mistakes that keep pieces from lining up properly. It is helpful to trace the adjoining sections of the birdfeeder roof onto the pattern first. Work toward the large branch. The grain direction changes in some areas. Cut the veins in the leaves, stopping just before you cut the entire way through; it's easier to shape the leaves first, then complete the cuts separating the leaves.

7 **Shape the leaves.** Start with the leaf that fits into the roof, lowering it to the roof, but not below it. You want the leaf to look like it's in front of the roof. The next one will appear to be under the surrounding ones. Mark the contour of the shaped leaves on the next ones to be shaped as you go. I use a smaller sleeve on the spindle sander to give a concave look on some, and a flexible-drum sander on others to round them. Run your sandpaper through the veins to clear out the sawdust. Glue them all together.

8 **Cut the large tree branch.** To adjust the pattern for fit, align a copy of the large branch pattern under the project. Hold the pattern in position, and slide a piece of carbon paper between the pattern and project. The riser under the roof makes it difficult to trace with a pencil. Trace around the roof with a finishing nail or awl held at a 90° angle. Attach the pattern to the work piece, and cut along the carbon paper lines. Glue the branch together, and shape it as one piece. Glue the branch to the rest of the intarsia.

9 **Apply your finish of choice.** All pieces should be sanded smooth as you shape them. Inspect the pieces by both sight and touch to make sure they are smooth. Remove any sanding dust. Apply two coats of clear satin gel varnish. Use an air compressor to blow excess finish out of the cracks and a rubber dental tool or something similar to clean any remaining varnish out of the nooks and crannies. Glue the cardinals, goldfinch, small branch, and leaves to the main project.

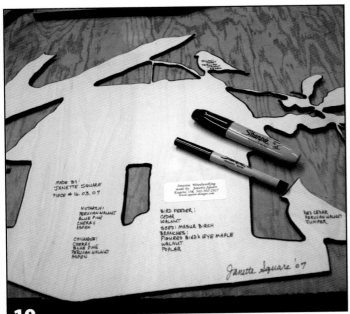

10 **Cut the backing board.** Trace the completed intarsia onto a piece of ⅛"-thick Baltic birch plywood. Use carbon paper and an awl when needed. Drill blade-entry holes to cut the negative spaces. Cut ⅛" inside the lines. Dry fit the backing board to the intarsia. Make sure the backing board isn't visible from the front, and sand it with 220-grit sandpaper. Color the edges of the backer with a black permanent marker. Sign and number the piece. I also list the woods I use. Glue the intarsia to the backing board and attach your hanger of choice.

Materials:

Woods:

- ¾" x 6" x 36" Western red cedar (assorted colors; bird-feeder, roof)
- ¾" x 6" x 24" walnut (birdfeeder, roof, knots of the tree, female cardinal)
- ¾" x 6" x 12" Peruvian walnut (branches, all five birds)
- ¾" x 6" x 12" blue pine (hook, chickadee, nuthatch)
- ¾" x 6" x 12" green poplar (leaves)
- ¾" x 6" x 24" figured bird's eye maple (branches)
- ¾" x 6" x 8" Tennessee red cedar (cardinals)
- ¾" x 6" x 4" juniper (beaks on all five birds)
- ¾" x 6" x 4" cherry (chickadee, nuthatch)
- ¾" x 6" x 4" aspen (female cardinal, chickadee, nuthatch, goldfinch)
- ¾" x 6" x 4" yellowheart (goldfinch)
- ¾" x 6" x 4" dogwood (female cardinal)
- ¾" x 6" x 4" Masur birch (birdseed)
- ⅛" x 18" x 24" Baltic birch (backing board)
- ⅛" and ¼" thick pieces of scrap (risers)

Other materials:

- Multiple copies of the pattern (for cut and paste method)
- Wood glue
- Assorted sanding tools, including 220-grit sandpaper
- Dowels, off-white acrylic paint (for eyes)
- Clear satin gel varnish or finish of choice
- Hanger

Tools:

- #7 reverse-tooth blade (most of cutting)
- #3 blade for cuts in between feathers (optional)
- Carbon paper
- Pointed tool to mark around intricate areas
- Air compressor to remove extra finish
- Rubber dental tool to remove extra finish
- Black permanent markers

Photocopy at 200%

Photocopy at 200%

Contributors

Nick Berchtold
Nick, of Illinois, started scrolling at age 16 and was designing his own intarsia patterns within a year.

Carol and Homer Bishop
Carol and Homer, of Illinois, enjoy cutting and designing intarsia patterns, some of which can be found at the following sites.
www.scrollerltd.com
www.woodenteddybearonline.com

Bob DeCuir
Bob, of California, a past president of the Scrollsaw Association of the World, worked with wood all of his adult life.

Frank Droege
Frank, of New Jersey, is an award-winning artist and author who enjoys painting and intarsia projects.
www.FoxChapelPublishing.com

James Haumesser
James, of Arizona, scrolls a variety of projects, but his primary interest is carousel horses.
www.creativecarousels.com

Mike Mathieu
Mike, of Virginia, runs Woodworking Plus and specializes in designing custom intarsia and intarsia project kits.
www.midlothianwoodworks.com

Susan Mathis
Susan, of California, loves and cares for all kinds of animals, which shows in her animal portraits.

Neal Moore
Neal retired from the Navy to West Virginia in 2002.

John Morgan
John, a school band director from Texas, enjoys playing his trumpet, spending time with his family, and cooking when he's not scrolling.
www.woodjam.com

Judy Gale Roberts
The author of numerous intarsia books, Judy, of Tennessee, is recognized as the leading authority on intarsia and was one of the first inductees into the Woodworking Hall of Fame.
www.intarsia.com

Dennis Simmons
Dennis, of Indiana, is a longtime woodworker and author of *Making Furniture and Dollhouses for American Girl and Other 18-Inch Dolls.*
intarsiawood@hotmail.com

Janette Square
Janette, of Oregon, made her first intarsia project in 2000. Her custom designs have appeared on the covers of woodworking magazines.
www.square-designs.com

Diana Thompson
Diana, of Alabama, is a prolific scroller and designer who specializes in compound cutting.
www.scrollsawinspirations.com

James R. West
James, of Louisiana, is an intarsia enthusiast who designs his own patterns.

Kathy Wise
Kathy, of Michigan, is a designer, frequent magazine contributor, and author of several books.
www.kathywise.com

Bruce Worthington
Bruce, of Michigan, designs a variety of intarsia patterns.
www.intarsia.net

Index

More Great Project Books from Fox Chapel Publishing

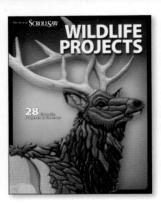

Wildlife Projects
28 Favorite Projects and Patterns
By Editors of *Scroll Saw Woodworking & Crafts*

Discover your inner Dr. Doolittle as you work on these all time favorite animal projects from the archives of *Scroll Saw Woodworking & Crafts.*

ISBN: 978-1-56523-502-1
$19.95 • 112 Pages

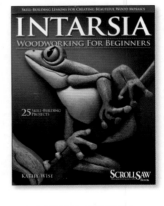

Intarsia Woodworking for Beginners
Skill-Building Lessons for Creating Beautiful Wood Mosaics
By Kathy Wise

You will learn everything you need to know to make beautiful intarsia artwork—from cutting basic shapes and sanding to stack-cutting and creating depth.

ISBN: 978-1-56523-442-0
$19.95 • 128 Pages

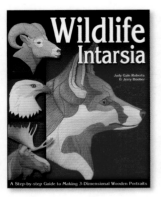

Wildlife Intarsia
A Step-by-Step Guide to Making 3-Dimensional Wooden Portraits
By Judy Gale Roberts and Jerry Booher

Learn to create beautiful wood inlay art for North American wildlife, including a wild mustang, bull moose, and bald eagle. Includes tips for simulating fur, and all the basics for getting started.

ISBN: 978-1-56523-282-2
$19.95 • 128 Pages

Animal Portraits in Wood
Crafting 16 Artistic Mosaics with Your Scroll Saw
By Neal Moore

Learn the technique of scrolled mosaics with step-by-step demonstrations and patterns for 12 North American animals.

ISBN: 978-1-56523-293-8
$17.95 • 128 Pages

Custom Wooden Boxes for the Scroll Saw
Innovative Techniques and Complete Plans for 31 Projects
By Diana L. Thompson

Learn the basics of making beautiful wooden keepsake boxes—including tips on tools, wood choices, and finishing techniques from noted designer Diana Thompson.

ISBN: 978-1-56523-212-9
$17.95 • 112 Pages

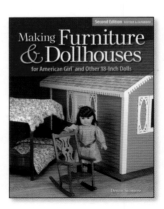

Making Furniture and Dollhouses for American Girl and Other 18-Inch Dolls
Second Edition, Revised & Expanded
By Dennis Simmons

Create a dollhouse and furniture with charming details for the American Girl® and other 18" dolls using easy-to-follow instructions.

ISBN: 978-1-56523-402-4
$24.95 • 200 Pages

SCROLL SAW
Woodworking & Crafts

In addition to being a leading source of woodworking books and DVDs, Fox Chapel also publishes *Scroll Saw Woodworking & Crafts.* Released quarterly, it delivers premium projects, expert tips and techniques from today's finest woodworking artists, and in-depth information about the latest tools, equipment, and materials.

Subscribe Today!
Scroll Saw Woodworking & Crafts: **888-840-8590**
www.scrollsawer.com